CRUISIN'

CAR CULTURE IN AMERICA

Michael Karl Witzel and Kent Bash

MBI Publishing Company

First published in 1997 by MBI Publishing Company, 729 Prospect Avenue, PO Box 1, Osceola, WI 54020-0001 USA

MBI Publishing Company books are also available at discounts in bulk quantity for industrial or sales-promotional use. For details write to Special Sales Manager at Motorbooks International Wholesalers & Distributors, 729 Prospect Avenue, PO Box 1, Osceola, WI 54020-0001 USA.

Library of Congress Cataloging-in-Publication Data
Witzel, Michael Karl.
      Cruisin': car culture in America / Michael Karl Witzel and Kent Bash.
         p.   cm.
      Includes index.
      ISBN 0-7603-0148-4 (hardcover : alk. paper)
      1. Automobiles—United States—History. 2. Automobiles—Social aspects—United
States. I. Bash, Kent. II. Title.
TL23.W588   1997
303.48'32—dc21   97-30403

On the front cover: A classic Main Street cruisin' scene punctuated by two quintessential boulevard denizens, a Pontiac GTO and 1934 Coupe hot rod. Mass-produced street racers entered the scene in the mid-1960s igniting a fierce rivalry between traditional hot rodders and muscle car devotees. *Kent Bash*

On the frontispiece: Car club plaques allowed cruisers to quickly identify street rivals. *Kent Bash*

On the title page: A speeding pack of muscle machines hauls down Detroit's Woodward Avenue, one of America's classic cruising strips. In the sixties and seventies, Woodward was home to endless street racing. *© 1997 Tom Shaw/Musclecar Review Magazine*

On the back cover: Top: The challenge. Calling out a likely competitor at the local eatery is a time-honored street-racing tradition. Racing was always in earnest with anything from cigarettes to pink slips as the winner's prize. *Kent Bash* **Bottom:** For cruisers the destination was often as important as the journey. Any evening of cruising had to include a break for a burger and a Coke and some socializing. *Courtesy Albert Doumar*

Edited by Zack Miller
Designed by Katie Finney

Printed in Hong Kong

Contents

Dedication

This book is in memory of Dave Wallen and dedicated to East Belknap Avenue, a once-vibrant cruising strip located deep in the heart of Haltom City, Texas. During the waning years of the seventies, I imagined that this linear representation of the American dream could be conquered with relative ease—as long as one possessed a cool car, a full tank of gas, and a blaring eight-track tape deck.

From its unofficial starting point at the sprawling complex of buildings that once housed Haltom High, it rolled right past a hodge-podge of "we tote the note" used car lots, commercial sales outlets, and third-rate motels. Within the first tenths of this miracle mile, the Belknap drive-in and its buffalo-bedecked screen (my alma mater's football mascot) announced its presence as *the* place for entertainment, socialization, and back-seat romance. At one time, I even worked there, flipping burgers and popping corn.

As the crossroads of Highway 377 zipped past, the asphalt followed a bead into the more urban section of town. There, the cacophony of wholesale and retail continued. Restaurants that were just beginning to steal the thunder from curb service stops became the unofficial landmarks: a vintage Arby's wearing multicolored cowboy hat neon and a Weinerschnitzel sporting a high-pitched roof. I reserved my unsophisticated palate for more basic car food, however: greasy cheeseburgers, fries, and a Coke.

With a languorous speed limit of just 30 miles per hour, Belknap straightened and sauntered past a Clownburger drive-in on the left and Griff's burger bar to the right. One and a half miles and four stoplights later, the ribbon of pavement unfurled a shameless path through a crazy jungle of juke joints, sleazy strip clubs, liquor stores, barbecue stands, greasy spoon cafes, second-hand furniture outlets, vacuum cleaner repair shops, and an ample assortment of porcelain-clad gasoline stations (I was awarded a pair of speeding tickets along this unforgettable stretch).

Beyond this illuminated mayhem of roadside commerce, bathed in the warm rays of flickering neon and the mournful sounds of a twanging pedal steel guitar (country and western music ruled in this part of town), the two-lane corridor dipped, curved, and slipped gracefully into the darkness. Overhead, a discordant highway overpass and its steady din of traffic marked the gateway to downtown Fort Worth and its deserted side streets. Here, a 180-degree turn was indicated to get back to the action. The busy cruisin' strip was over; East Belknap had run its course.

The Haltom City, Texas, cruising strip known as East Belknap Street was the driving destination of choice during the sixties and seventies. Today, it's just an alternate route heading into downtown Fort Worth. *Mike Witzel*

6

Foreword

I wish I had a dollar for every mile I cruised in my lifetime. If I did, I could retire and spend the rest of my days wrenching on hot rods and going on rod runs. No doubt about it, I've driven millions of miles going nowhere and doing nothing special. Sounds crazy, but that's what cruising is all about: driving for the fun of it. Showing off your car, looking for races, or better yet, looking for girls, was all a part of the action.

Egos were big during the fifties and sixties, and if you were cool and had a nice car, you had to cruise around your high school in the morning and after school to show it off. Despite the fact that I lived less than 100 yards away from my high school, I drove there in my car anyway just to "make the scene." It was an adolescent ritual that everyone followed.

I was fortunate enough to own two nice cars at the time, and they were both pretty well known by the entire school. In one of these, we would cruise to the high school football games on Friday nights. When we saw a good-looking girl walking to the game we would "shoot her a rev" to get her attention. It worked every time. Then, if her response was favorable, we would pick her up and give her a ride, or we would try to locate her at the game or the sock hop that was held after the game.

We also cruised the local hot spots around town. One of the most action-packed was King's Ice Cream Parlor. The location was a great one, right in a shopping center that had a record shop and a movie theater. Since all the local kids hung around the ice cream store and record shop, it was a natural place for cruising. Most of the girls that hung out there were hoping some fellow with a nice car would want to meet them. The cute ones were very, very successful; I can vouch for that.

Drive-in restaurants were also perfect places for cruising. In the southern California area, Bob's Big Boys were the top spots. Most of the kids who lived in the northern areas of the San Fernando Valley, a Los Angeles suburb, cruised Bob's Big Boy in San Fernando. Although every weeknight it was loaded with cars, on the weekends it was extremely busy. This particular Bob's had two lines you could get your car into: one for a parking spot that had car service and another just for cruising through!

Some of the nicest cars would cruise through, go around the block, and cruise through again. This could go on well into the night. It was like a revolving car show. The Bob's Big Boy in the town of Van Nuys was even better: At this location, a seemingly endless stream of hot rods and customs cruised through the lanes, and seldom did you see the same one. The line of cars that were waiting for service or cruising stretched out for a good number of blocks. At the busiest times, it wasn't at all unusual to be in line for an hour or more just to pick up a hamburger!

It sounds simple, but there was much more to cruising than just driving your car through a restaurant parking lot. There were unwritten rules you had to obey. First of all, you had to be cool doing it. If you owned a hardtop, all the windows had to be rolled down and the radio or Muntz four-track stereo had to be full blast. At the same time, you had to sit low in the seat. If it was a convertible, the top had to be down. If you were cruising through a drive-in after dark, your headlights had to be turned off the minute you got in the cruise line. If you were driving a custom, hubcaps were fine if they were Fiestas, spinners, Caddies, Moons, or chrome wheels with baldies, but if you were driving a stocker, the hubcaps had to come off (before leaving home), because otherwise everyone would accuse you of driving "Daddy's car."

A "good" cruiser never sat at its stock height either. In the early sixties, your car had to be low. After the muscle cars came out, it became acceptable to raise your car a little, just as the Super Stock racers of the era did. You also needed a dual exhaust setup with glasspack mufflers, so your car sounded really tough. If you were a member of a car club, the plaque had to be prominently displayed.

When you cruised through a restaurant, it had to be done very slowly, and you had to check everyone out while you were doing it. Some of the really cool custom guys even cruised with their shades on at night. If you were cruising with your girlfriend, she had to be sitting right next to you, even if that meant that she had to sit on the console! If you didn't follow the rules, everyone would know you were a novice cruiser. Not cool.

Many of these rules applied to cruising Van Nuys Boulevard, the ultimate cruising strip in the San Fernando Valley. This was one of many streets in southern California crowded with kids cruising and having a good time. Hawthorne Boulevard was another favorite in the South Bay area, and Whittier Boulevard was also a popular cruising strip. And there were countless others. People cruised these boulevards for a host of reasons, but the obvious ones were to check out the cool cars, show off your car, and try to get into races. Ultimately, though, most guys and gals cruised for social reasons.

Young fellows cruised for chicks, and the gals looked for guys. Cruising provided a chance to meet people who didn't go to your high school. Friday and Saturday night were hot, but Wednesday night was known as "girl's night" and the boulevard was packed. For a cover story, girls would inform their parents that they were going to a "girl's club meeting." Later, after the meeting, they went cruising! As they arrived, the guys were already there waiting to "pick up on them."

Here are the basics of the ritual: You cruise onto Van Nuys Boulevard, ending up in one group of traffic. If you spotted a carful of girls, you then tried to wind your way through cars until you were right next to them. If they looked good, you would strike up a conversation and make plans to meet them at Bob's Big Boy, or another location. Most of the time these "meetings" took place in front of the Praisewater Funeral Parlor, the only section of boulevard that wasn't lined with shops; it was more like a small park and became the favorite meeting area. If you didn't like any of the girls in your group of cars, you would cruise around the block one more time and join another group of cars to start the search all over again.

Some of the races run on the boulevard started the same way, except the flirtatious exchange was replaced by some guy making a sarcastic remark about your car. The manly thing to do was "blow his doors off." But most of the cool guys wouldn't choose-off another car on the boulevard; they would go to the parking lot where street racers hung out. That's where the real racing action was taking place, for money. Guys who tried to start races out on the boulevard were usually high school nerds driving Daddy's car for the night.

Ah, the good ol' days. We were all having fun with cars and really didn't have a care in the world. Without a doubt, it would be fun to relive those days. Unfortunately, all of it changed during the mid-sixties, and it hasn't been the same since. For those who would like to take a trip into the past and experience that way it was, *Cruisin'* provides a comprehensive look at how cruising evolved, the cruising heydays of the fifties, the muscle car influence of the sixties, a look at contemporary boulevard action, and a prediction of what the future holds for cruising. Read on and learn all about it. Me? I'm gonna turn up the radio, lay a patch of rubber, and cruise off into the sunset.

—Jeff Tann, editor, *Rod & Custom*

Acknowledgments

Thank you to all of the car nuts, gearheads, grease monkeys, automaniacs, customizers, hot rodders, shade-tree mechanics, and motoring maniacs who assisted with time, advice, knowledge, and materials. The top eliminators: Howard Ande, Bill Aufman, Jerry Bryant, Steph Butler, Martin Cable, Frank and Sondra Campbell, Randy Chadd, Pat Chappel, Eunice Christianson, Gil Clayton, Dan Daniels, Joseph DeRenzo, Michael Dregni, Albert Doumar, Fred Dupuis, Peggy Dusman, Sue Elliott-Sink, Wolfgang Fanth, Tic and Kay Featherstone, Mike Fennel, Howard Frank, Robert Genat, Robin Genat, Margaret Gifford, Scott Guildner, Serena Gomez, Mike Goyda, Shellee Graham, Frederick B. Group, Tab Guildner, Richard Hailey, Mark Hamilton, Dan Harlow, John Hutinett, Joan Johnson, Parker Jones, Dave King, Max Klaus, Gary and Diane Lick, Derek Looney, Harold Looney, Joe Loprino, Ron Main, Cliff Maxwell, Jerry McClanahan, Bill and Cindy McClung, Duncan McIntyre, Richard Mclay, Mike and Cindy Morgan, Bill Norton, Tom Otis, Brett Parker, Clare Patterson Jr., Dalton Patterson, Steve Perrault, Louis Persat, Wes Pieper, Ed Potthoff, Don Preziosi, Mike Rascoe, Halvin "Jackrabbit" Releg, David Rodarte, Ted Roen, Jerry and Linda Rogers, Mel Santee, Perry Schafer, Tom Shaw, Robert Sigmon, Charles F. Smith, Andy Southard, Gary Spaniol, Larry Spaniol, Mel Spaniol, Harry Sperl, Alice C. Stewart, Mel Strong, Jeff Tann, Clark "Crewcut" Taylor, Paul Taylor, George and Beverly Tibbs, Jeff Tinsley, Bud Toye, Cheryl Travers, Charles Vandreason, A. J. Vogel, Dave Wallen, Mike Wallen, "Slim" Waters, J. Frank Webster, Steven Weiss, Anthoula White, Jerry White, John White, June Wian, Tim Wisemann, Joe Van Witsen, Gyvel Young-Witzel, Brock Yates, and Hervez Zapata. Finally, a special thank you goes out to all the organizations that assisted with various photographic images and research, including Applied Images Inc., American Automobile Manufacturers Association, American Petroleum Institute, Automotive Hall of Fame, Burbank Historical Society, Chevron Inc., Circa Research and Reference, George Cross and Sons, Inc., C. W. Moss Auto Parts, the Library of Congress, Dallas Public Library, Detroit Public Library National Automotive History Collection, Douglas Photographic, Henry Ford Museum and Greenfield Village, the National Archives, Personality Photos, Phillips Petroleum Company, Security Pacific National Bank Photograph Collection of the Los Angeles Public Library, Steak n' Shake Inc., University of Louisville Photographic Archives, and the University of Southern California Library Whittington Collection.

Introduction

I Feel the Need for Speed

The urge for vehicular movement begins young; the influences that guide our subconscious toward "automotive frenzy" are first encountered in our youth. During this formative period, our minds take in a vast variety of stimuli, analyze the information, and store it for retrieval at some later date.

It's no wonder children can't wait to get their feet on the accelerator pedal! Since the early days of the wheel, mobile contraptions have colored a baby's first trips into the outside world. After successfully entering the world, attendants wheel the infant from the delivery room on a gurney, where it is most likely placed in a basket mounted atop four tiny wheels. Some might argue that the first fuzzy images a child sees are the happy, smiling faces of parents, but there's no denying the influence of the dizzying blur of ceiling and lamp fixtures whizzing past the baby's eyes as it makes the rounds from delivery room to newborn ward.

Once the child is transported home, the introduction to vehicular movement is further reinforced. The car trip home becomes the first pleasing experience of mobility. As Dad takes the automobile up to speed, the engine begins to hum, and the gentle rocking motion over the roadbed mimics the environment within the womb. Enclosed in the vehicle's protective shell, the child lies face up staring at a headliner and dome lamp as an entirely new world rushes past the windows.

Within days, parents treat the new arrival to a host of adventures, by means of a variety of wheeled contraptions. First comes the standard baby carriage. The fledgling gearhead lies recumbent in a kind of open coach—a roadster if you will—guided by its parents. Much like a hot rodder running along the dry lake beds, the child cruises along the sidewalk, safely tucked in and wearing a knit-weave crash helmet and a woolen-

Hot rod rides enjoyed for a nickel were perhaps some of the first automotive experiences children remember. Unlike a smooth riding car, these rides—with their exaggerated movements and sound effects—provided a fertile base for the imagination to form its own opinions about speed and motion. Even at such an early age, the desire for a better street machine begins. No doubt this toddler is pointing at a better ride just down the midway of this Pine Brook, New Jersey, auction market. *Author portrait/courtesy Karl Witzel*

blanket safety belt. A parent's firm grasp on the handlebar is the only brake to stop its forward movement.

But while the baby becomes the center of attention for friends and relatives, the carriage often takes on as much significance as the newborn itself. Always on public parade and demonstration, this simple child transporter becomes the outward indication of the parents' prosperity, social standing, style, and personality. The infant's "ride" functions as the predecessor for all four-wheeled status to follow, whether the tiny passenger is aware of it or not. Long before we utter the word *car*, the competition for speed and beauty has begun.

Parents who earn a decent wage can afford the luxury of pushing little junior down the avenue in the finest of perambulators. Automotive-like features such as a landau roof, convertible top, removable sunshade, rubber tires, ball-bearing hubs, spoke wheels, adjustable undercarriage, parking brake, chrome-plated trim, tufted upholstery, removable mattress, and a spring-cushioned suspension are some of the extras that leave budget baby carriages in the dust. Coincidentally, most of these features translate to the automobiles of later years.

In the final analysis, it's our parents who unknowingly prepare us for the attack of "automania" that occurs during adolescence. There's a good chance our folks have dragged, dropped, and driven us in almost every kind of rolling contraption while we were still very young. We are completely powerless to resist the draw of internal combustion and movement. By the teenage years, the wheel has become another extension of our body, and we are ready to assume ownership of mobility and embrace it fully. It's time to cruise.

Directly and indirectly, children are taught the wonders of the automobile from the time of birth. In the imaginations of the young, it's quite easy to turn a home-built go-cart into a full-house street machine. Today, as it always was, this is the seed behind the entire hot rod movement. *Kent Bash*

14

America's Heyday for Hot Rods

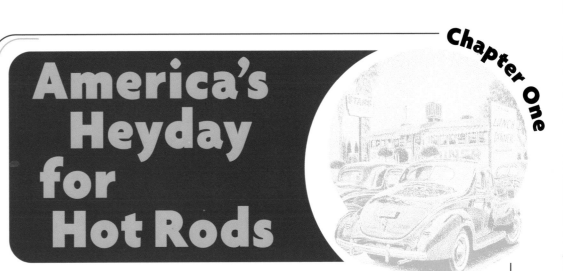

Forming the Obsession for Cruising

"I remember my older brothers buying their first car together when I was around six or seven years old. It was the early fifties, and there was this guy living up the street who had an old automobile—I think it was a Nash or a Willys—sitting there on the curbside near his house. It sat there gathering dust for a few years, just begging for a new owner. Hot for the road and for girls, my two brothers were destined to buy it.

Dangerously close to the legal driving age and eager to get behind the wheel, my brother Gary walked down and talked to the guy about the possibility of him selling his relic (it hadn't been fired up in years). At first, the man wasn't keen on the idea, and he started bragging about how he would eventually fix the thing up. Little did the guy know that this was precisely the plan my brother had—sort of.

Fortunately, the neighbor changed his mind and agreed to sell the old clunker. The asking price was a grand total of 10 bucks. My brothers pooled their cash, and after a handful of dollar bills were exchanged, they became the proud owners of their very first set of wheels. Excited by the prospect of cruising around town in their new prize, they pushed the bomb home. There in our driveway, they began work on reviving the dead engine with a devotion that bordered on mania.

As it turned out, it took a lot of tinkering and tweaking to get that baby running. What's worse, the junker didn't even have floorboards in the back seat. No big deal—they just patched the holes by welding in a few pieces of scrap metal! Jury-rigged repairs were the standard of the day. No other option existed really. There simply weren't many places for a gearhead to pick up resto parts such as fenders or interior trim. To fix up a ride and personalize it, you picked up a few more cheap wrecks as donor cars and towed them home. Stuff was removed from one car and added to another. If the pieces you needed didn't match up with your jalopy, they were just cut to fit!

In those days, kids didn't have access to store-bought parts, aftermarket goodies, or other repros. During the fifties, guys like my brothers, who were wigged out on cars and had a burning desire to bolt together their very own hot rod, relied on good old-fashioned American ingenuity to get rolling. The fact that a guy was broke and unable to buy parts wasn't a handicap at all. Lack of money was the mother of all invention and creativity."

—Kent Bash

Throughout the decades, the businesses involved with the repair and modification of automobiles have provided the fertile breeding grounds for all manner of hot rods and custom cars. Since materials and equipment were readily available, shop down time was put to good use, resulting in lookers like the flamed 1932 Ford Roadster and gleaming 1951 Mercury shown in this scene. *Kent Bash*

Chapter One

AMERICA'S cruise craze reached a frenzy during the fifties and, like a juggernaut on wheels, kept right on rolling. Postwar society regarded the modern-day, motorized equivalent of the horse-drawn carriage a necessary element of every person's life—a gadget essential for all manner of employment, travel, and recreation. The prosperity that followed World War II created an exceedingly amicable climate for cars, and the automobile transcended its more obvious uses and rose from the streets to become a distinct part of American culture.

The cult of the American teenager and the culture of the automobile were racing toward each other at high speed—head on. When they finally collided in the streets, motorists felt the impact nationwide, and before all was said and done, the sounds of squealing tires and rumbling mufflers reverberated from coast to coast.

Both the auto and the automobilist were changing. Kids were snapping up old cars, tinkering with the engines to make them go faster, reshaping the bodies to make them look sportier, and reworking suspensions to achieve an altered ride. No longer an afterthought, paint became a dramatic way to display one's style. Motoring the drives of Detroit and the lanes of Los Angeles, one could witness the metamorphosis: Cruisers reworked their cars to reflect the changing attitudes of a new generation. Suddenly, the accepted standards of mechanics and design were being rewritten as a new form of vehicular jazz. High

By 1925, three out of every four cars in America were being purchased on the installment plan. More and more people could get in on the American dream and with little or no money down look as if they were doing better than they actually were. At the same time, the popularity of golf surged, and it seemed everyone was taking up the sport and putting on the outward appearance of prosperity. Car makers responded with a roadster revival to lure this sporty crowd into showrooms. Later, these two-door convertibles would become the body style favored most by America's first hot rodders. *From the collections of the Texas/Dallas History and Archives Division, Dallas Public Library*

notes were being hit across America and the virtuosos of the genre coined a new phrase to describe their driving passions: *hot rod*. Christened by the collective consciousness of a nation and baptized with mechanic's sweat, a new variation of the automobile was born that all at once was loose, wild, hip, and racy.

According to the late Dean Batchelor, automotive journalist extraordinaire and author of *The American Hot Rod*, "any production vehicle which has been modified to provide more performance" may be classified as a hot rod. Though that defined hot rods in the early years, it might be more inclusive to say that a hot rod is any engine-dominated vehicle that breaks accepted rules and invents new ones. Forty years ago, that's precisely what returning servicemen were doing. Landing in the shore cities of California, they returned with practical, hands-on experience in the disciplines of aircraft design and engineering. Unlike shade-tree mechanics who understood only the functional basics of cars, these ex-servicemen possessed valuable experience in the design principles that made it all work. To their credit, they applied the knowledge to the creation of automobiles.

Because of the proliferation of good roads, a year-round mild climate, and the vast availability of second-hand cars, California quickly became the number one breeding ground for these future hot rodders. In light of the fact that California led the rest of the nation in the ratio of population to motor vehicle registrations, it wasn't extraordinary that the West Coast became the hot bed of American automotive activity. As far back as 1929, the statistics were already raising eyebrows: For every two and one-third residents, one motor vehicle was wheeling down the street! When the automobile manufacturing industry compared this ratio to the national average, they categorized the California market as the "bottomless pit" of automotive sales!

Although hot rod historians acknowledge that the modification of cars and their engines probably occurred around the same time nationwide, it was the Golden State that nurtured the movement into a full-blown obsession and made it a cultural phenomenon. As experimentation with modified vehicles took place, California operators made plans to serve all the smoking, sputtering hoards motoring down the pike. Car-oriented

businesses of all types sprang up: In 1929, Harry Carpenter built a series of drive-in restaurants in Los Angeles and before too long, it seemed that everyone thought of eating and driving as the same thing. Drive-in shopping centers sprouted, along with drive-in theaters, drive-in dry cleaners, drive-in banks, and even drive-in car washes. By the time hot rods gained notoriety during the fifties, roadside businesses provided the self-sustaining loop: Additional cars created more commerce, and additional commerce created more cars.

Without a doubt, all of those heaps and hot rods clogging the streets made the notion of cruising around in a car difficult to ignore. Plus, the image of the decadent hot rodder leaving a trail of madness and mayhem in his wake was just the ticket for those young people wishing to stir up the

The 1950s was a great time to be a kid and a great time to learn about the joys of owning an automobile. In America's sprawling suburban settlements (like the one that sprouted in California's San Fernando Valley), streets and sidewalks were busy with all sorts of vehicular activity. Foot-powered bicycles, tricycles, and scooters vied for space as pedal cars like this fetching police cruiser (driven by future street cruiser Mike Wallen) zipped along the sidewalks in search of automotive fun and adventure. It's ironic that the same kids would one day be pulled over by the cops while cruising. ©1997 Dave Wallen

In 1928, the nation was high on the automobile and every available hour of leisure time was spent in pursuit of activities within vehicles. This "human hood ornament" pose is a perfect example of the giddiness of the era. Pictured here is actress Sally Blane, a player for Paramount pictures. The vintage ride is an Oldsmobile Landau sedan. *The Automotive Hall of Fame*

older set's emotions. In September 1955, actor James Dean personified the defiance felt by an entire generation of teens and aptly portrayed the rebellion in film. Although the establishment didn't know it then, *Rebel Without a Cause* marked a turning point in the hot rod movement, with the doomed misfit Dean cast as the speed-loving, drag-racing, chicken-playing troublemaker. At long last, the hot rodders-turned-juvenile-delinquents had their poster boy.

In an uncanny twist that became automotive irony, Dean met his untimely death three days before producers released the movie. While driving his Porsche 550 Spyder on Highway 46 near Paso Robles, California, another vehicle crossed his path on a wide curve and the two crashed—with fatal results. In the frenzy of posthumous adulation that

A MONOGRAM PICTURE
with
JAMES LYDON

Art Baker · Gil Stratton, Jr. Gloria Winters · Myron Healy

roduced by JERRY THOMAS · Directed by Lewis D. Collins Screenplay by Dan Ullman

"Spindizzies," or toy racing vehicles that employed miniature internal combustion engines to make them go, were one of the more exciting types of car toys for children who grew up during the twenties and thirties. Without a doubt, toys like these set young imaginations to wonder what it would be like to drive at high speeds in a real car. *Courtesy Jerry Bryant*

followed, teenagers began to covet the freedom and mobility afforded by the motor vehicle more than ever before—whether their parents approved of the idea or not. The car, and especially the hot rod, was crazy, sexy, and cool.

To be fair, impressionable adolescents of the era had no choice over their drive-in destiny: A seemingly endless parade of billboards, magazine advertisements, radio programs, television commercials, and popular films assailed the senses with automotive propaganda. In mainstream periodicals such as *Life* and the *Saturday Evening Post*, one couldn't turn more than a few pages before catching sight of a gleaming new machine. Oil companies sponsored the latest radio and television programs, and shows like the *Texaco Star*

Theater promoted gasoline consumption. The gas station attendant became a friendly assistant, one who filled your car with the fuel needed to motor out to the local drive-in theater or movie palace. There, virtually every motion picture featured a combination of new cars and hot rods.

By the time Dwight D. Eisenhower signed the American Highway Act of 1956, teenagers were hypnotized by automobiles and the allure of driving. Everyone was. As work on more than 40,000 miles of modern, concrete, four-lane "limited-access" highways began, America's adolescents desperately clutched at the wheel to log as many miles as they possibly could. Indoctrinated by more than 15 years of training in baby carriages, strollers, tricycles, bicycles, pedal cars, and the various "motor toys" of childhood, there was no way to deny them a place behind the wheel.

Since the early 1900s, American family photo albums and personal scrap books have been characterized by happy images of people sitting in their automobiles or standing somewhere near them. However, no documentation of the long journey to one's automotive independence can be complete without a snapshot of Junior and his first motoring machine, the pedal car. The teenage years—and the hot rod yearning that they inevitably bring—are waiting only a few miles down the road. *Courtesy John Hutinett*

Going on a cruise with the entire family was one of the main leisure activities for the nuclear family of the 1950s. The car provided the means to get wherever Mom and Dad wanted to take us—whether that was on a vacation, a trip to Grandma's house, or down to the local shopping center. *Courtesy American Automobile Manufacturers Association*

Spec Sheet

HOT ROD DICTIONARY

QUARTER—quarter mile

RAIL JOB—an all-out dragster, because its frame is made from thin tubing.

TRAPS—area at end of strip where speed and elapsed time are measured.

WIPED OUT—to b

get your complete HOT I
eck offer on back of wrapp

SERIES 1 NUMBE

**GET MORE OUTS
PICTURES EVER**
est HOT ROD - DRAGSTER
7"x10" Full color pin-up
HOT ROD magaz

ET YOUR COPY
ORITE NEWS D
ad $3.25 by check or mo
10 month trial subscr
HOT ROD MAG
PT. BGL 5954 HOLLY
LOS ANGELES, CALI

HOT 5c
ROD
BUBBLE GUM

OD DICTIONARY

and 5 Hot Rod
Bubble Gum wrappers for your
HOT ROD DICTIONARY to:
HOT ROD DICTIONARY
P. O. BOX 2838
MEMPHIS, TENN. 38102

**HOT ROD
DICTIONARY**

DONRUSS CO., MFR., MEMPHIS, TENN. MADE AND PRINTED IN U.S.
GUM BASE, SUGARS, CORN SYRUP, NATURAL AND ARTIFICIAL FLAVOR
AND U.S. CERTIFIED COLOR. CONTENTS 1 SLAB BUBBLE GUM AN
PICTURE CARDS. © B.L.W.

The culture of the hot rod had such a pervasive effect on the popular culture of America during the fifties and sixties that all sorts of products took advantage of the theme. In addition to a wad of chewing gum, kids got great trading cards of neat rods and a lot of inside info on the back. *Courtesy Mike & Cheryl Goyda*

Regardless of race, color, creed, or social standing, this unceasing urge to "go mobile" became a universal phenomenon among our nation's young people (it remains so today). "When I was a kid I just couldn't wait to get my driver's license," reminisced Jeff Tann, editor of *Rod & Custom* magazine. "I bought my first car, a Model A Ford, when I was 14 years old and

would sometimes sneak it out when my parents weren't home. I would cruise the 'A' on the local back streets of my neighborhood and check out all the other hot cars in the area. In the process, I met a lot of older guys who told me about all the great cruising spots they'd been to. When I was finally old enough to get my driver's license, I already knew where all the best cruising places were, and naturally I had to visit each and every one."

Not surprisingly, Tann's cruising experience is not unique. Most males who grew up during the fifties succumbed to the siren song of the internal combustion engine, and some even decided to make it their life's work. Even as early as the thirties, more progressive high schools across the nation had added to their curricula a new type of industrial arts course known as "auto shop." Initially viewed as an elective intended to train those individuals without plans for college, it proved to be a salvation for countless kids who harbored childhood dreams of building a car that looked hot and ran fast. Kids enrolled in droves just so they could get their hands on some *real* tools, like hydraulic hoists and other tools of the trade

Contrary to popular belief, auto shop enrollees weren't dumb. While some lacked the patience for "book learnin'," many proved their mettle in the mechanical arts, and for them auto shop became a place where they could learn practical, tangible skills and get immediate feedback from their efforts. Young men (and a few women) worked with their hands and mastered the techniques required to construct hot rods of their own design. Engines, exhausts, body panels, and bumpers became the outlet for excess energy. Future gearheads and drag racers spent time rebuilding carburetors and packing their fingernails full of grease while high school socialites (more commonly referred to as "soshes") crammed for college entrance exams and memorized algebraic equations.

Present-day hot rodding enthusiast and restorer Wolfgang Fanth was one of those hot rod hopefuls. "When I was goin' to high school back in '54, hot rods were the one thing I dreamed about most . . . next to girls," he claimed. "I practically lived in the garage of our school's shop, and so did a lot of other guys. One May afternoon, I dozed off under a 1932 Ford heap I was fixin' up and woke to find that all the lights had been turned out. Everyone had split! I ended up stayin' all night until I got the gearbox I was workin' on put back together." For parents and teachers, it was incidents like these that defined the teenagers' strong points of view when it came to their cars.

Of course, there was whole a lot more behind the car fetish than just the hankering to waste after-school hours avoiding homework and zigzagging aimlessly around town. The obsession for motors and cars took root in the compulsion to make contact with the opposite sex! As envied as they were, those spoiled preppies whose parents

Future hot rodder Mel Spaniol taking the first steps to building a Model A roadster in the growing bedroom community of Woodland Hills, California, circa 1954. After the work was completed, the vehicle was hand painted with a brush, the young hot rodder's tool of choice when it came to affordable paint jobs. *Courtesy Mel Spaniol*

Mel and Gary Spaniol, two brothers and fellow hot rodders who knew a good deal when they saw one. The 1935 Willys in the background was the first car they bought, purchased from a neighbor down the street when Gary turned 16. This was the age of the $10 car, a carefree time when wheels could be picked up on the cheap, and no one imagined that a car would one day cost as much as a house. *Courtesy Gary Spaniol*

had the resources to purchase the newest model Chevrolet convertible for their offspring knew the score; without a doubt, a cool car was a prerequisite to get girls and to get laid. If that car was a racy, sexy hot rod, one had a good shot. So car owners became aware of the numero uno reason for cruising: Driving an awesome automobile was the most effective way to attract females and keep their interest—far from the prying eyes of parents and other adult authority figures. While parked out on Lover's Lane, the "submarine races" at the lake, or right in the parking lot of the town's drive-in movie theater, the automobile provided the young and the restless a portable, private compartment to act out the tentative night moves of youth.

At the same time, the car and all of its wonderful trappings supplied a ready outlet to vent the effervescent emotions of the teen. That's where the hot rod came in. While at the controls of a boss heap, drivers expressed sexual and aggressive urges by stomping down on the accelerator pedal. The result? Instant power and immediate gratification. Furthermore, the car provided rambunctious juveniles a highly visible way to rebel against their elders (both at school and home) and even enabled the unpopular fringe to show off among peers.

The simple possession of an automobile imbued the American teen with more than just ownership status. The automobile was a magic carpet ride that promised to fulfill every fantasy. The simple acts of sliding a key into the ignition, turning over the engine, and pulling out into traffic, allowed young adults to transform themselves into something that they weren't, to mimic the personalities of their heroes, or build an entirely new legend of their own choosing.

Most kids who grew up in the postwar era didn't have a lot of money, and the cars they built were sometimes never finished. At cruise nights, cruisers like Fifties Dan, spark the memory and remind those who drive today's ultimate cruisers of their hot rod roots: primer paint jobs, blanket seat covers, missing parts, and engines that were constantly being repaired and overhauled. *Kent Bash*

Hidden away in garages and barns and owned by little old ladies and crusty old curmudgeons, hot rod stock like this 1930 Model A awaited discovery by budding cruisers in small towns across the land. Before these cars became collectibles, hot rodders found little trouble and little expense in talking their owners out of them. Doing all of the work required to make them over into a hot street machine was the hard part. *Kent Bash*

Abandoned by their original owners, future hot rods and custom automobiles began their second lives in America's junkyard. Although it's acknowledged by scholars that fifties "assemblage" artist John Chamberlain first used the scrap of junked cars as sculpture material for his three-dimensional artwork, cruisers would be happy to inform you that it was the clique of unruly hot rodders, the clans of customizers, and the cool lowriders who first rearranged the discards of America's scrap heaps into meaningful, motorized art. *Mike Witzel*

As a birthplace for hot rods, this Wisconsin garage was just like countless other automotive shops strewn across American during the thirties. In places like these, motor mechanics had all of the tools necessary to create the fast, cool cars that existed only in their imaginations. Mechanics working in shops like this ushered in a dramatic new automotive era. ©1997 Dave Wallen

For parents, age 13 is when the trouble usually began. It had all started out quite harmlessly with father allowing junior to "steer" the car when he was just a toddler. Over the years, this innocuous activity developed into a constant wailing to control the wheel. By the age of 15 or 16, overly anxious teenagers were officially ready to learn how to drive and parents instructed them on how to do it. From the driveway and beyond, unschooled drivers had to endure frantic yelling, horrific contortions of the face, screams to "put on the brakes," and crazed howls of fear to "slow down!" For the sake of cars and cruising, they persevered. When a student driver was finally ready to go down to the motor vehicle department to take the driving test and win his or her learner's permit, it was a grand occasion indeed—exceeding the importance of birthdays, Christmas, and all the other holidays in between. With both the written and the physical driving test passed, all the waiting was over. Once kids gained possession of the signed slip of paper from the testing officer's pad, the joys of the automobile became readily accessible. Hot rod hell was keeping a back burner stoked and ready for all new arrivals. The only remaining activity was finding access to a car—any car!

Unfortunately, borrowing mother and father's stodgy four-door sedan, pickup truck, or Woody left many socially conscious kids wanting more. Since buying a new vehicle was almost always out of

the question (for the average kid), so-called "used cars" became a teen's first automotive purchase. There were a lot to choose from, since Detroit had sold 6,326,528 brand-spanking new cars in 1950 alone! During the decade of dazzle, General Motors rolled out 26,215,080 shiny new machines restyled to reflect the optimism of the era. By then, America's motor market was ready, willing, and able to buy, and it wasn't long before soaring tail fins, gleaming chrome, and wide whites took up driveway space. Finally, those worn-out flivvers that saw motorists through the lean years of gas

rationing and conservation joined the funeral march to the scrap heap. At last, old motoring stock became freed up—allowing every grease monkey to construct a hot rod and go cruisin'.

With little pomp and ceremony, the mid-forties ushered in the age of the jalopy. By 1948, there were well over 8,000 scrap and junk wholesalers selling and parting out defunct cars in the United States! Somewhere, out there—waiting for resurrection—were the battered hulks of long-forgotten sedans, touring coupes, and roadsters. Stacked high amid the mud and weeds, America's youthful

En route to the Pacific, World War II servicemen shipping out for duty passed through southern California. When they returned from overseas, they brought back a variety of talents in mechanics. After they settled in the region, it didn't take long for these skills to be transmuted to cars. Across driveways, mechanics shared information with their neighbors. Fathers passed down car knowledge to their progeny, as if it were a family history to be revered. Similarly, the groups of teens huddled around drive-in restaurants passed on auto wisdom to all who would listen. Eventually, even schools began holding classes in "auto shop." *John Collier, Library of Congress*

car nuts rescued them from the acetylene torch and car crusher. Along the roadways less traveled, junkyards overflowed with the rusting remnants of forlorn Fords, memorable Mercurys, derelict DeSotos, and crunched Cadillacs—all were excellent pickings for prospective car builders eager to find their diamond in the rust. While in the establishment's view the junkyard was a cemetery for discarded clunkers, young people knew better. For them, the junkyard was a place of promise, the nursery for hot rods, and the primordial soup from which all the great motoring machines to come would soon be born.

So, with learner's permit in pocket or driver's license clutched tightly in hand, the youth of the late forties and early fifties ventured off in search of an acceptable vehicle. As they delivered the newfound prize to its home and dragged it up on the suburban housing tract like a beached whale, mothers peered out from their kitchen windows and fretted about the grease tracks while fathers wrung their hands over the blocked driveway. One-time bomber plant riveter (and mother) Eunice Christianson recalled those days with marked trepidation: "My son Johnny was eat up with that hot rod thing. I'll never forget the day he came home all covered with dirt and grease and oh, so happy as a lark. He was just grinning from ear to ear, beaming over the jalopy he and his friends had just bought at the junkyard 'cross town. My, oh my, the driveway was ruined after that, and my husband had no end of trouble trying to keep the mess from spreading! Until John joined the service, I can't remember one time when there wasn't an old beat-up wreck out there dripping grease all over the place." Drunk with the thoughts of gearshifts, gasoline, and girls spinning

around in their heads, proud Johnnys all over the country were digging into their toolboxes—oblivious to the reactions of disbelief.

All across America, would-be mechanics raised hoods and rolled up their shirt sleeves. The youthful segment of car culture had begun the great experiment. Inspired by the same muses that once guided the coachbuilders of the automobile's golden age, they proceeded to imagine, conceive, and eventually (if they could find all of the parts) construct what they thought a really "neat" car should be. With a couple of years of formal training in the technical arts of the automobile (and some didn't have that), it was nothing more than an overwhelming feeling of self-determination, a few heartbeats of hopeful talent, and plain blind luck that aided their haste to become mobile.

Never mind that the heaps and hot rods that rumbled, lurched, and sputtered forth from the depths of suburban garages, filling stations, and back alleys of America were the direct opposite of the factory-assembled standard. Even though these homemade cars never attained the refinement of mass-produced vehicles, they were by no means less attractive in the mind's eye of those who built

During the forties and fifties, the 1928-1931 Model A Roadster was one of the most accessible and affordable vehicles to use when one was thinking of building a hot rod. For a teenager who desired to go mobile, all it took was a few visits to the local junkyard to uncover treasures that had been dreamed of for so long. More often that not, the vehicle created would only be a shadow of what one might own 30 years later. *Kent Bash*

Although these days it's become more difficult, discovering a Model T Touring Car like this rusting relic was the genesis for many a hot rod project in the fifties and sixties. To the uninitiated, this useless hulk may have looked like just so much scrap metal. But to a hot rodder, it was a precious find that only required some hard work and ingenuity to transform it into a prized possession. *Kent Bash*

The Ford Model T bucket roadster provided hot rod enthusiasts a visible showplace for their detailed engine work. Reworked and reinvented from discarded motoring stock once rusting in junk heaps and forgotten garages, chromed jewels like this 1927 roadster personify the dramatic transformation of a car from the category of junker to classic cruiser. *Kent Bash*

them. To their creators, achieving the ultimate car design wasn't the point. More important was the perception that claptrap jalopies could be as liberating, captivating, and magnificent as the finest factory-assembled car. With that realization, builders laid down one of the important creeds of cruising for generations of motorheads to come: You really don't need a pot of money to put together a really bitchin' hod rod. When it comes to the hop-up built from the ground up, teamwork, industriousness, and a little ingenuity go a long way in beating out the big money.

As the urge to build rods spread from the California coast to the rest of the United States, certain vintage models rose to prominence among hot rodders. During the formative years of the movement, enthusiasts cruising the fringes didn't get excited about two-door coupes and four-door sedans. It was those inexpensive, lightweight roadsters stamped out by the Ford Motor Company (in great numbers) that cruisers chose. Originally intended for the sporty set, the jaunty roadster became a protean base for the hot rodder's speedy aspirations. It was lightweight (important for racing), small, and had a four-cylinder engine that almost anyone could rework. For a brief time in hot rod history, it came to define the whole era of the $10 car.

But while the Model T and its four-cylinder "mill" dominated the rodding arena for years, the Model A eventually came to define the hobby's look. When it debuted in 1928, 788,572 units made it to the streets in the first year! The reasons for its popularity were many. Engineers had incorporated 20 years of improvements into its design and it contained 5,580 new parts! Standards that motorists admired in the energetic T went to a new level. New additions

In limbo, a 1927 Model T body rests on a 1932 Ford Frame. Not every hot rod project started by young cruisers managed to make it to the streets. When building a hot rod back in the fifties, money was often in short supply and more than a few cruising dreams were put on permanent hold. *Kent Bash*

included hydraulic shocks, four-wheel brakes, a gasoline gauge, and an automatic windshield wiper. Under the hood, a redesign of all moving parts and major components made the car's mechanical workings much more substantial. Plus, expanded engine bore and stroke added a boost in performance, providing 40 horsepower from the factory.

As speed freaks of the Depression years clamored to see what kind of power they could extract from the revamped four-cylinder, Ford engineers

For the teenager bent on building a hot rod or street machine, under the hood is where most of their time was spent (when not cruising). Short on funds but long on enthusiasm, young car builders often exhibit an unusually long attention span when it comes to tinkering with automobiles. Is it any wonder that high school auto shop was such a popular course of study? © 1997 Dave Wallen

worked on an entirely new powerplant for the line. After four years of research, groundbreaking manufacturing processes allowed technicians to cast an eight-cylinder engine block as one piece. Henry Ford released this revolutionary valve-in-block "flathead" for the 1932 model year. With just a few modifications, this mill would become the reigning favorite of hot rodders during the coming decades.

In a letter dated April 10, 1933, infamous bank robber Clyde Champion Barrow related his great satisfaction with the product to Henry Ford: "I have driven Fords exclusively when I could get away with one . . .," he penned. "For sustained speed and freedom from trouble the Ford has got ever [sic] other car skinned and even if my business hasn't been strictly legal it don't hurt enything [sic] to tell you what a fine car you got in the V-8."

To placate the loyal customers who helped the Ford company grow during the early years of the Model T and the Model A, Ford introduced the Model B at the same time the flathead rolled out. Although it used the same basic body and trim work as the V-8 variation, the Model B featured an upgraded version of the Model A's four-cylinder engine under the hood (with 10 extra horsepower to

The ever-present "jalopy" was a common sight during the formative years of the cruising obsession. During the twenties and thirties, worn out flivvers like this one could be seen in almost any town and on almost any street. Teenagers everywhere were sowing their wild oats via the automobile. *Courtesy Karl Witzel*

One of the more long-lived hot rod styles is the "highboy," typified by a 1932 (or earlier) fenderless body that's mounted atop the frame. In comparison, the "lowboy" features a body shell that is *lowered* over the frame by channeling (the floor is cut out and raised). This classic beauty was captured at a cruise along Route 66, the Mother Road. ©*1997 Robert Genat*

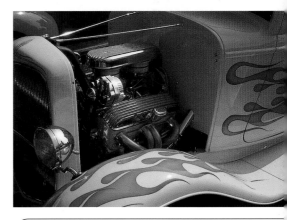

Seen parked in front of the Wigwam Village Motel (made famous along Route 66), this cool purple hot rod (a 1929 roadster highboy) is a graphic example of the classy, simple, sublime hot rods that have become so popular among today's cruisers and hot rodders. *Kent Bash/car owned by Bud Toye*

Unlike the ordinary motorist who accepted the fact that his or her automobile should have the same brand of engine as the body, hot rodders and customizers harbored no such preconceived notions. Depending on one's preference, Chevrolets might have had Ford engines or vice versa. Here, a 1932 Ford body and chassis provides a snug home for a powerful Chevrolet engine. *Kent Bash*

its credit). Bolstered with heavy-duty rod bearings, oil pressure supplied to the main bearings, and a counterbalanced crankshaft, the reliable four-banger had more bite than ever. To its credit, all of the bolt-on "speed equipment" that was compatible with the first Model A engines worked with this new model as well! Nevertheless, this was not the model that later achieved hot rod greatness.

For aesthetic reasons, the 1932 V-8 flathead Ford (roadsters, phaetons, sedans, and three- and five-window coupes) broke ahead of the pack and leaped the quarter-mile stretch to finish as the hot rodder's main machines during the fifties. Although the subtle details were not readily discernible by those outside of the car hobby, the 1932 became prized by hot rod enthusiasts for its looks. In contrast to the Model A, it flaunted a more graceful grille and, according to many, had improved lines. Company designers managed to better integrate the fenders and the hood with the body—attaining a

more pleasant-looking passenger carriage. "There's not one thing that you can put your finger on that makes the '32 a favorite," said Kent Bash. "The whole design of the car just works!"

Because of the numeral *2* in its model year, a hot rod made from this mass-produced series of cars became known in car circles as a "deuce." At that time, people often used the term deuce (or "devil" as Webster's defines it) as a cuss word when expressing anger. Since the aesthetics that were evolving to define the looks of a hot rod were taking on a rather devilish look themselves, the nickname proved to be more than a slang term for members in-the-know. The American hot rod was definitely the devil incarnate. How else would one describe a car that had a chopped top, no fenders, fat rear tires, angled rake, no bumpers, exposed engine, and flames painted on the side?

During the early years of motoring it was all the rage to tie foxtails to the rear-view mirror, paint humorous slogans on the body side panels, and maybe even mount a novelty hood ornament; but the naive trends that defined accessories during the twenties and thirties were no longer fashionable after the war. Although arriving at high school football games sitting in the rumble seat wearing a funny straw hat and thick beaver coat might have been "23 skidoo" for dear old Dad, practices seen as scandalous 20 years prior became the hokum of present day. For the postwar teenager, everyday life was getting faster and more complicated. As a byproduct of progress, "kicks" were getting more difficult to find. The hot rod—or modified car—provided thrills with an amplified version of horseplay that spelled fun for almost every adolescent.

FULL FREQUENCY **STEREO** FULL FREQUENCY

The new music and sounds of the Hot Rod set

K-417
GRAND
PRIX
SERIES

HOT ROD
LINCOLN
— CHARLIE
RYAN

Gas Heat
Valve Grinder
Cam Shaft
Fleet Mills
Skins
Shute
Off The Line
Tube Steak
Puffer

35

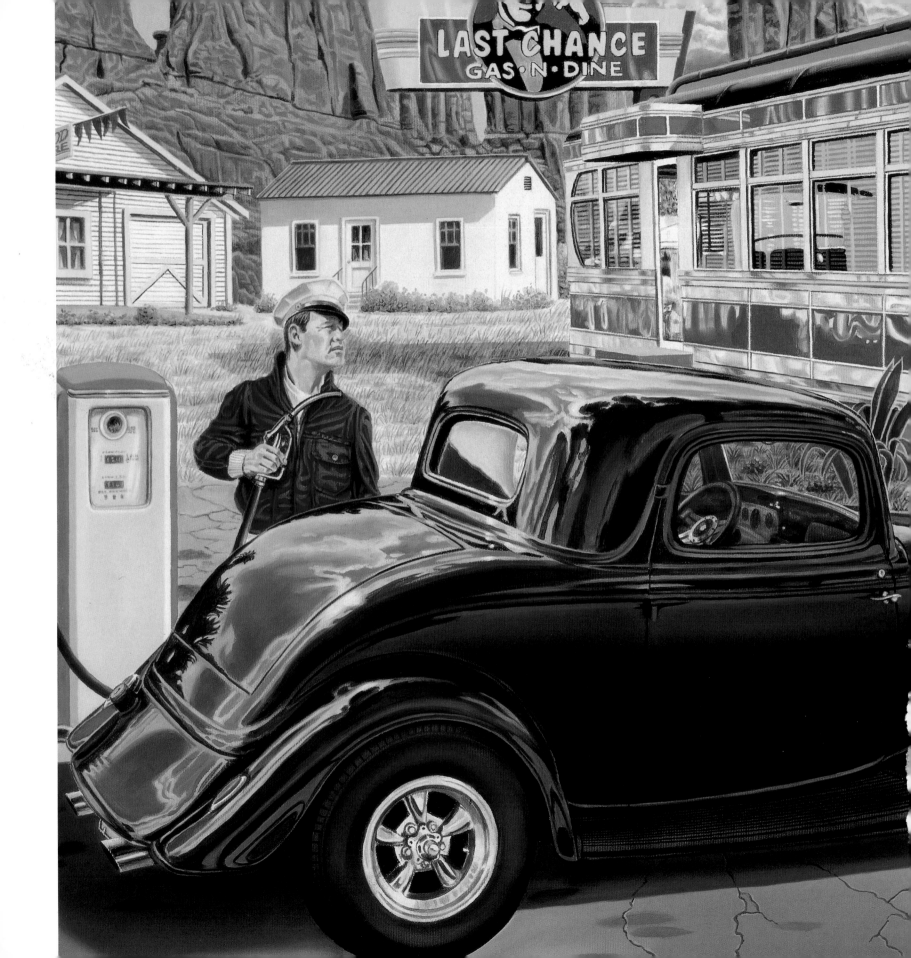

Historically, the diner has been an East Coast phenomenon, but on occasion, one may be seen in more remote parts of the country. The driver of a 1934 Ford three-window coupe running American mag wheels and 1939 Ford taillights (with the popular teardrop shape) stops at this Western dream for gasoline, a cup of Java, and maybe even a cup of chili. *Kent Bash*

THE DEUCE COUPES
THE SHUT DOWNS

WITH MY BABY ★ 36 THREE WINDOW COUPE
TWO FASTEST CARS ★ BODY BY FISHER
TURN HER ON, BUDDY

STARTERS NIGHTMARE ★ OIL ON THE TRACK
GOIN, GOIN, GONE ★ GOGGLES GOT A HOLE IN IT
DEUCE COUPE

With songs like "Goggles Got a Hole in It," the fifties album by the Deuce Coupes was a resounding favorite of the hot rod and custom crowd. The only problem with owning the album was that it couldn't be played in the car. Cassette decks and compact discs were the talk of science-fiction. *Courtesy Mike & Cheryl Goyda*

High-performance cars added a whole new arena of misbehavior for cruisers to indulge in. It was bad enough when cruisers created noise, harassed commuters, instigated traffic accidents, and ran rampant over public and private property; but when they tired of these shenanigans, they turned their wild wheels into instruments of sport! Behind the wheel of a hot rod, drivers issued spur-of-the-moment racing challenges to "opponents" with relative ease. Cruisers acted on racing offers while waiting at the traffic light, fill-ing up a tank at the corner gas station, or getting a bite to eat at the drive-in restaurant. From there, two wild-eyed teenagers floored it and shifted through the gears, putting both life and limb in jeopardy (of themselves and others) in a conspicuous attempt to affirm their driving skills, technical aptitude, and creativity.

At the finish line, the battle for supremacy yield-ed only one clear winner, harking back to the early days of civilization when hunter-gatherers showed their power by way of the hunt and battles with com-peting clans. The temporary flush of victory felt after a race or the feeling of dominance gained by owning a nifty heap was all part of the prize. Call it bravado, cajones, guts, or just blame it on an overabundance of testosterone—the fact was that the hot rod came into being because of the age-old instincts that spur boys to compete and prove themselves. As true today as it was in the past, the force behind the hot rod movement was the American male's need to display his prowess by way of the automobile.

Of course, automobiles and hot rods weren't just the domain of boys. There were some girls who liked hot rods and hot cars, too. During the fifties, so-called "B" movies with evocative titles such as *Dragstrip Girl* and *Hot Rod Girl* quickly stereotyped these car-crazy gals as wild vixens who were "Hell on wheels . . . fired up for any thrill!" Evocative movie posters depicted these "crazy kids . . . living to a wild rock 'n roll beat!" as jiggling blonde bombshells dressed in trampy, skin-tight dresses and sweaters. As their boyfriends raced for supremacy at the local drag strip, they pranced around in high heels with their skirts hiked up way too high and their breasts jostling out of control. Not surprisingly, most parents of the time were mortified by the shameless images being portrayed, and they circled the wagons against the evil hot rodders.

To counter this youthful braggadocio and keep it from going off the rails, a groundswell of opposition formed against all of the racing, cruising, carousing, and crashing that gave hot rods so much bad press. Along with the police and local government, parents became the most vocal adversaries of the hot rod menace and discouraged (or forbade) kids from even building hot rods. To them, rodding was a waste of gas and a quick path to trouble. Religious leaders agreed with the analysis and, in due time, rallied against the excesses of cruising: One prominent preacher who was traveling with a motorcycle daredevil show during the heyday denounced the revelry as "a fast track to Hell." He went on to proclaim that if an accident didn't snuff out your life, eternal damnation would condemn you by way of "the immoral practices indulged in in the back seat"

Although most of the police, parents, and Bible-thumpers who opposed hot rods and fast cars didn't even tune into the same top-40 radio stations as their adversaries, the tension between the old and new generations was manifest in song by 1955. That year, Charlie Ryan and the Timberline Riders debuted a rock and roll

tune called *Hot Rod Lincoln* (Ryan really owned a 12-cylinder Lincoln). In the song, a kid driving a Model A passes cars "like they were standing still" out on Grapevine Hill and then proceeds to blow a Ford and Mercury right off the road. Later, he passes a Cadillac sedan and a new race begins. This time, the hot rod kid develops engine trouble and the cops pull him over. In the final words of the song, the point of view shifts from the racer to the parent who laments, "Son, you're gonna drive me to drinkin' if you don't stop drivin' that hot rod Lincoln." Summarizing the establishment's basic attitude toward fast driving and cruising, the tag line proved to be a somewhat prophetic statement.

Unfortunately, cruising forced many parents to hit the bottle for relaxation. By that time, the hot rod—and the myriad forms of car culture that it had spawned—had contaminated the hearts and minds of youth from coast to coast. The establishment's troubles were just beginning. Over the next 20 years, teenagers would take over Main Street, invade the drive-in restaurants, affect our native tongue, change the course of automotive design, create new rolling art forms, make love in the back seat, do battle with the law, build bigger engines, create a new racing motor sport, waste more gasoline, and have no end of fun doing it all. The best—or worst—of America's cruising craze was yet to come!

In a 1957 issue of *Life* magazine, cruiser Norm Grabowsky and his $8,000 rod were featured in an article about hot rodding. The combination of polished chrome, flamed paint job, "skull" shifter knob, and drive-in food tray somehow caught the imaginations of kids all across the nation. After the tabloid hit the racks, everyone went nuts over his car, including the producers of the television series *77 Sunset Strip*. In the program, Edd "Kookie" Byrnes was to be a carhop who owned the beautiful roadster. Of course, television exposure caused even more people to desire one of those beautiful roadsters and "Grabowskyitus" spread over the highways and byways. A reproduction of the famed "Kookie" car is shown here. *Courtesy Gary Lick*

Cruising the Main Street Strip

Myth and Mayhem Along the Urban Boulevard

"When Friday night finally rolled around, my friends and I hit the roads with a vengeance! It was a wild mix of cars, girls, drive-ins, bowling alleys, racing, rock and roll music, and all of the other pastimes kids growing up during the early sixties loved. The circuit we picked out for cruising was a particular favorite: This night was the one reserved for taking in the sights and sounds found along the mother of all American cruisin' strips, California's Van Nuys Boulevard.

To start the fun we cruised to the teenage hub of activity, the San Fernando Bob's Big Boy drive-in restaurant. From there, we followed the trail of neon lights all the way down Sepulveda Boulevard and hooked a left onto Parthenea to connect up with the bustling Van Nuys strip. The next stop we made was Oscar's Drive-in, a roadside hangout where they fixed a really good triple-deck hamburger and a spot where a bunch of "greasers" always hung out. While this drive-in wasn't as well known in the area as Bob's, the parking lot was always packed with cars. We didn't stay there long, slowing down just long enough to check out the action.

Once we finished the cruising loop through Oscar's lot, we continued rolling south along the main artery of Van Nuys and past all the major businesses. Sometimes, we hung left at Victory and stopped at Cupid's walk-up for a hot dog. Eventually, we ended up at a second Bob's Big Boy drive-in and queued up in a snaking line to get a parking place for curb service. During the long wait, there was ample opportunity to listen to rock and roll music on the car radio, check out the chicks, other hot rodders, and anything else that was interesting.

On the final leg of our Friday night cruise, we drove out to the Toluca Lake Bob's Big Boy. With no thoughts of resting, we drove hard into the night, cruising to the Colorado Boulevard Bob's in Glendale, California. Still eager to run through a few more of the drive-ins, we doubled back to Hollywood and made the obligatory drive-by at the famous curb stand known as Tiny Naylor's. Satisfied that we had hit all of the major hot spots, we slipped down Sunset Strip and returned to the spot where it all began: the Van Nuys Bob's. By then, we were pretty much inebriated with images of hot rods and cool customs dancing in our heads and were ready to call it a night."

—Kent Bash

During the height of the cruising craze, scenes like this one were a common sight. Back then, marques like Lexus and Infinity didn't even exist and automobiles like the 1958 Chevrolet Impala and Corvette ruled the street when it came to good looks and class. In the days when hamburgers were made with 100 percent ground beef and milkshakes were mixed up with real ice cream, the accepted aesthetics of the automobile were different. *Kent Bash*

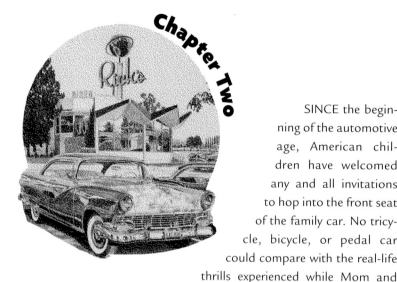

Chapter Two

SINCE the beginning of the automotive age, American children have welcomed any and all invitations to hop into the front seat of the family car. No tricycle, bicycle, or pedal car could compare with the real-life thrills experienced while Mom and Dad were at the wheel. Lacking all thoughts of commuting to work, car payments, insurance and repair bills, the automotive journeys of youth were always an unspoiled pleasure. More important than the destination, the ride was the focus. Among these many-splendored trips taken in the motorcar, the outing glorified as the "Sunday drive" was often the most memorable—and adored—of childhood.

Unfortunately, those innocent automotive adventures of childhood don't last forever. Advancing maturity causes us to change our priorities. By the teenage years, raging hormones bring on an awareness of "self." Suddenly, those once carefree attitudes of childhood become clouded with self-conscious thoughts. As a negative side-effect, the compulsion to sustain a presentable image (constantly) begins to distort the personality. Impressing the reigning teen peer group becomes the most important activity in life. Being seen by one's friends while seated in the back of Mom's old Windsor Town and Country station wagon becomes a major embarrassment—a bittersweet reminder of our toddling years on training wheels. Really, there was only one way to portray an image of cool and sustain it: own your own automobile.

Main Street provided the central corridor for the cruiser and became the strip where much of the automotive action took place. During the fifties, Saturday nights were reserved for the motorized activities of youth and the downtown strip became the "conspicuous gauntlet" for cruising one's car. This sign was spied right off of old Route 66 in Luther, Oklahoma. *Mike Witzel*

"I was really fortunate," explained Clare Patterson, now an avid cruiser and owner of a Cool Mint custom 1955 Chevrolet coupe. "Since we lived out on a farm in Augusta, Kansas, my dad said that I needed a car to get to school! During my freshman and sophomore years I put over 60,000 miles on my '50 Chevy convertible. During that time, we lived only 6 miles from town! On my 1954 Ford (it had only 17,000 miles on it when I bought it), I racked up 110,000 miles during my junior and senior years. . . . My dad just could not understand how I put so many miles on that car!" For cruisers like Patterson who came of age during the fifties, there were many good reasons to turn over the odometer numbers by cruising around.

In those days, the motorized art of looking cool was the top priority. While slung low into the seat, donning a pair of dark Wayfarers (with a pack of Camels rolled up in your shirt sleeve), one hand firmly grasping the suicide knob, and the right foot planted nervously on the gas pedal, there were so many exciting places to go and so many good reasons to go there alone. The high school sock hop or the Friday night football game played across town (and the wild festivities that often followed) were not events one wished to be taxied to! Furthermore, "parking" for a romantic evening or taking in a movie at the drive-in theater (with a date) didn't lend itself to Mama chaperoning in the front seat, either. For those under legal drinking age, it proved difficult to explain why they needed a ride to the liquor store or to the seedy honky-tonk where friends were gathering to catch the latest rockabilly band. Besides, how could a boy salvage his reputation after the fastest guy in town laid down a challenge to race while Mom was behind the wheel?

For these reasons and a glovebox crammed full of a thousand more, America's inventive teenagers formulated a new type of motoring trip to replace the weekend outings once enjoyed with

the family. Although the motorcar was still the method of conveyance, there were a few distinct differences: Instead of being used as a medium for keeping the family together, the car became a personal, private compartment for socialization, amusement, and escape. Automobiles provided teenagers with a self-contained environment that went wherever the action was taking place—whether it was on the move or standing still!

The central street of any American city (large or small) became the most exciting stretch of blacktop. This was the traffic lane known as Main Street, a corridor that hosted the myriad activities of cruising.

Until freeways became the corridors for commuters and travelers alike, the commercial avenues of transportation criss-crossed their way through the center of town. Often, Main Street became part of a major thoroughfare, and consequently, it was packed with businesses attempting to reap the bounty of commerce. After high-speed highways like this one in Los Angeles (1949) were built, many towns were bypassed and the action on Main died. The mega-mall and shopping center on the outskirts of town began a slow takeover. *Library of Congress*

In the far and distant days before the advent of the shopping mall, Main Street was the place where it all happened for the cruiser. On one stretch of centrally located street, one could take care of all the business of living and at the same time find various forms of entertainment. Of course, the car provided the means to get there and to make it all happen. It was only a natural progression for teenagers and young adults (with cars) to adopt it as cruising heaven. ©1997 Dave Wallen

As would be expected, the Main Street that was seen during the day was different than the Main Street that materialized after dusk. When the sun dipped below the horizon and traffic lights took prominence, the strip was transformed. Like clockwork, the authority figures that ran their shops behind the panes of glass locked the doors and doused the lights. When the neon twists of streetside signs flickered to life, the traffic lanes were reborn. Like ravenous ants vacating their hive, four-wheeled creations of every make, model, and description streamed in to get a chance to run the conspicuous gauntlet. ©1997 Dave Wallen

Long before the advent of the shopping mall, Main Street was where the people congregated to conduct the transactions of life. At its starting point, where the rows of houses changed into commercial structures, the filling station occupied a place of prominence. There, car nuts hung out, pumped gas, and gave birth to hot rods (for fifties teens, landing a job as a station attendant was a major coup). Further down the sidewalk where the parking meters sprouted, townspeople patronized the butcher, baker, and green grocer. Along the way, the red-white-and-blue barber pole was a familiar sight. Anyone who desired a flattop, ducktail, or pompadour took a chair there. Clothing and shoe stores lined the strip, too—along with five-and-dimes like Ben Franklin and Woolworth's. Inside these emporiums, soda fountains and lunch counters beckoned customers of all ages to sample burgers, fries, pop, and malted milkshakes. At the opposite end of Main, the new car dealership was the place of dreams. Through panes of glass, a fantasy world of chrome and lacquer taunted shoppers with the promise of shiny new cars. For young people, everything along Main spoke of prosperity.

Since local residents had to visit Main at one time or another, cruisers driving slowly from one end of the strip to the other would likely see someone that they knew, or wanted to know. After dark, when the stores closed and all of the shoppers had gone home, the atmosphere for automotive carousing became electrified: Flashing light bulbs, neon lights, blinking traffic signals, and glaring street lamps transformed the commercial corridor

into a brightly lit automotive stage. Like colorful, strutting peacocks, cruisers arrived from all points to brave the conspicuous gauntlet.

As a diverse cast of car characters vied for an opportunity to appear on the linear stage, the Main Street venue provided a common ground where both similar and dissimilar car groups could meet and rub bumpers. Everyone was there: greasers, gearheads, socialites, athletes, book-worms, and troublemakers. All comers took their

turns with equal enthusiasm. This was no longer the Main Street that Sinclair Lewis wrote about in his sentimental novel of the same name during the twenties. Now, the gaslights blazed as bright neon and the horse-drawn carriage was replaced by the power of the piston. Main Street had become more than just a place to buy goods. It was now a place to have a good time.

While the merchants locked their doors and parents peered out their windows in anticipation

California's famous Pan Pacific auditorium (now defunct) provides an appropriate Art Deco back-drop for two chrome-bedecked 1959 Dodges and a 1956 Corvette. Ever since the first cars were designed, body styling and commercial architec-ture have followed similar courses. When art deco was in vogue, car bodies followed the cues of industrial designers and featured rounded shapes and elaborate embellishments. Later, when the architecture along Main Street became more angular, automobiles shared the form. *Kent Bash*

of trouble, cruisers wrote a new chapter on having fun in the streets. Most of it was pretty tame stuff: While parading up and down Main, kids found recreation in ogling pedestrians, harassing shoppers, yelling to friends, and making a general nuisance of themselves. When traffic was heavy, the kids packed their cars full and when they stopped for a light, all the doors flung open as the occu-

pants jumped out from the car! In a "musical chairs" fashion, participants ran around the vehicle in circles until all the players got back in the car through another door. When the light turned green, the "Chinese Fire Drill" was over and the player who ended up in the driver's seat slipped it into gear and sped away. On a more sinister note, some teens adored nothing better than a really gory practical joke, including the old standby where a bloody rubber arm poked out of the trunk. What did the cruiser do in this scenario to raise eyebrows? He drove around town asking for directions to the nearest lake!

Without thinking, some cruisers engaged in the creation of even more hard-core mischief and mayhem. "We would drive off of the road at night with the lights turned off, just to see how far we could go until we ran off of the road," explains Paul Taylor, publisher of *Route 66* magazine. "We played chicken a lot! When another car was coming down the road, we drove down the same side that they were approaching, until the last minute. Eventually, one of the cars had to give up, and hopefully it was the other guy. We even played it out on the highway, running farmers off the road until they drove into the woods or down into a ditch!" Where were the kids getting the ideas for these unbelievable antics? While a good part of it was born of youth's innate creativity, most of the blame pointed to the moviemakers in Hollywood. Classic "out of control" flicks like *Running Wild* and *Hot Rods to Hell* were some of the influential primers behind the unsavory behavior.

But there was more. When cruisers weren't causing accidents, kids who were getting their kicks in cars engaged in all sorts of other malicious fun. While waiting at an intersection for the light to change, it was great sport to have someone sneak out of the car and deflate the rear tires of the motorist waiting ahead. Occasionally, the vehicle vandalism bordered on the silly: Having a windshield creamed by roving marauders who were carrying cans of shaving cream was common. In times of boredom, a well-positioned potato stuck up the muffler of some unsuspecting Joe's automobile (usually the school principal or some other authority figure) was just the ticket to create a few moments of laughter.

Embarrassing others was a great hobby for the car-crazy kid, too. In that department, "mooning" was an effective way to turn blue-haired grandmas' faces red and make girls scream. By pulling down their pants (or hiking up their skirts) and pressing their bare buttocks against the car window or thrusting them out into the open air, rebellious teenagers could embarrass their victims with great aplomb. The message to rival cruisers passing by: "Kiss my ass!"

Whether or not acts of malice or juvenile pranks defined the cruisin' trip, the destination was universal for most all of the participants. A majority of the Friday night tours taken in an automobile shot straight through a city's heart. In a driving "loop" that extended for miles from the north and south poles of Main Street, the meandering paths that defined the cruising circuits changed according to individual taste. Drive-ins, diners, and ice cream stands defined both shape and direction. To ensure maximum exposure, participants piloted their cars between the most visible landmarks—saving the slow roll along the downtown strip for last. The cruisers who drove the entire loop turned a quick 180, powershifted through the gears, and repeated the exhibition—until the gas, money, or night ran out. Since fuel was an unbelievably cheap commodity, cruisers fed their craving continuously. Well into the wee hours, the kids just kept coming back for more!

California's Ventura Freeway became one of the world's most traveled freeways during the 1970s. As a superhighway that followed the mountains and separated the San Fernando Valley from the beach areas, it became one of the main thoroughfares for West Coast cruisers commuting to work and play. For the cruiser, it was a vital link to all of the many feeder roads where the drive-ins (and fun) could be found. *Kent Bash*

Historically, small town gasoline stations like this extant example in Yoder, Kansas, were the hub of mechanical activity when it came to teenagers and their hot rods. While working there pumping gas, it seemed there was always time to put in a few extra hours on one's own machine. *Mike Witzel*

Parked at a circa 1937 gasoline filling station on the outskirts of town, this Ford five-window coupe and its lovely occupant make an order for gasoline and service. During the early days of pleasure cruising, the act of taking a car to the gasoline station was part of the fun of driving. Attendants in those days wiped the windows, checked the oil, and really took care of the customer. Today's cruisers can only look forward to self-service. *From the collections of Henry Ford Museum and Greenfield Village*

There was good reason for the attraction to the bright lights and excitement of the cruising loops: the goal was to meet members of the opposite sex. Main Street was one big singles bar, and naturally the male of the species flocked there in great numbers. With their hopes inflated by excess hormones, teenage boys who were old enough to pilot two tons of glass and sheet metal—but still too immature to figure out what a woman really wanted in a man—prowled the streets of this two-lane social club with the sole intent of "getting lucky." On a typical Saturday night in America, most of the young bucks who lacked dates but had

cars were trying almost every trick in the cruising book to win over girls and get them to hop into their chariots. And during the revved-up heyday of cruising, they put on quite a show.

Making a racket gained favor as an effective technique for the cruisers who wanted to call attention to themselves. While one waited at the stoplight, cranking up the radio volume was almost an instinctive reaction—especially if girls pulled up in the other lane. When rock and roll anthems like Elvis' *Heartbreak Hotel* or Jerry Lee Lewis' *Great Balls of Fire* seared the airwaves, there was no controlling the volume level. Revving up the Cherry Bombs (a glass-pack muffler)

Getting a job at a gas station during the teenage years was almost as great as dating the prom queen. With all of the mechanic's tools and other equipment available, the corner gas station at the end of Main Street became a virtual nursery for hot rods. In California, Michigan, Texas, New York, and all points in between, street machines of every description emerged from garages to do battle in the streets. With a cool car, one didn't need to be the most popular person in town or have the best looks; a jet-black, 1935 Ford three-window coupe with a chopped top and Halibrand wheels was really all that was needed to get a date with the gal of your dreams. *Kent Bash*

and pouring on the power until the car almost red-lined (also used at the drag strip to warm tires prior to a run) a smoky "burnout" came in second.

For older people watching from the sidewalk, the "display" activities of cruising were nothing less than infuriating. The only ones who appreciated the effect of pumping the gas pedal (to make a car surge to and fro), jerking the wheel left and right to create a wild "ride," or tapping the brakes at regular intervals to bring on a "staccato movement," were the participants themselves.

In spite of the male "machismo" that ran roughshod over the streets, having a good time while cruising wasn't only the domain of boys exercising their libidos. Cindy Morgan, a current cruiser with the Heart of Texas Street Machines (she explores the strips of the Lone Star state with husband Mike in a 1959 Pontiac Star-Chief) handily dispels the myth: "My very, very first car was a '66 Volkswagen, and we used to do like everybody else did and see how many people we could pile into it. Usually, we would have at least six or eight girls stuffed into a little Volkswagen drivin' around town, of course, tryin' to see how we could pick up the boys and everything!" From today's perspective, it was mostly harmless fun, since average girls of the age guarded reputations as important assets. So-called "good girls" seldom hopped into the back seat of the first deuce coupe to drive by, just because it had a dreamy paint job and chromed wheels. The reality of the situation was that finding a new flame while cruising wasn't that easy. Protected by the automotive shell, neither party pulled over and put it into park unless the amorous feelings were mutual.

There were a few select places where mixed crowds could mingle outside of the car safely, however. The drive-in restaurant was one of them. Main Street provided the primo place for people to show off their automobiles when moving; the drive-ins provided the best place to display motor vehicles when stopped. As the universal dating, meeting, and gathering spot for the many types of

Main Street denizens of Ellensburg, Washington, once had Wipple's gas station to cruise into when the gas gauge dropped toward the empty mark. In cities and towns all across the country, the scene was the same: At each end of the main traffic route, gas stations of every brand vied for cruisers and commuters alike. *Mike Witzel*

to make the statement, "Look at me, I'm here, I'm cool, and I'm really loud" was another standard practice. "We used to speed up at the big hill right before Main. As we came over the hump, we let up on the gas pedal to get the mufflers a rumblin'," mused Clark "Crewcut" Taylor, now the operator of a small exhaust repair shop in the West. "These days, making muffler noise is a long forgotten art. Nowadays, it's the loud, rap music and those amplified stereo radio systems with those subwoofer things and all that get the looks!"

Besides creating noise, there were other ways to gain the attention of bystanders. Since the car equaled self-image, boys proved the mechanical prowess of their hot rod by laying a "scratch," or long patch of tire rubber on the road. By stomping the brake pedal

At the turn of the century, the Coca-Cola Company promoted its syrup throughout the South with posters and point-of-purchase items that depicted people in their carriages being served by waiters. These runners were often employed by pharmacies of the age to carry out refreshing beverages to people waiting patiently in their horse-drawn coaches. Out of this practice came the drive-in restaurants and the legions of young men and women who cruised there in great numbers to get a drink. *Courtesy Coca-Cola Company/author's collection*

Unlike the average restaurant that concentrated its culinary craft on serious sit-down clientele, the Texas Pig Stands catered to car lovers who wished to remain inside their vehicles. At circular units like this example in Beaumont, Texas, dining away from home was both convenient and fun. Hot rod and custom car crowds especially liked the open-air atmosphere of the carhop service, and by the end of the fifties the drive-in became the hangout of choice for everyone who had access to a set of wheels. *Courtesy the Texas Pig Stands Inc.*

cruisers clogging the streets, drive-ins were at the height of popularity during the fifties and reigned as the preferred hangout until the mid-sixties.

Along with Main Street, drive-ins unified the cruise, providing those "shooting the loop" with convenient way stations with easy access and refreshment. Enthralled by the flamboyant carhops, the neon tubing, and the zesty food, the youthful sector of America's car crowd reacted to the atmosphere of the drive-in restaurant with overwhelming approval. Without walls and the various rules of

Drive-ins, diners, and coffee shops are all geared to serving people who arrive in cars. Before there were motor vehicles, restaurants were located in the downtown area—usually along Main Street—where the customers could get to them easily. As Americans became ever more mobile, dining establishments located themselves on the outskirts of Main Street where land was cheap and they could throw down a couple of acres of asphalt for parking. Shown are a 1957 Chevrolet Nomad station wagon, 1958 De Soto, 1957 Oldsmobile, and a 1958 Plymouth. *Kent Bash, courtesy George Cross and Sons Inc./Pomona Swap Meet*

behavior that accompany them, the atmosphere at America's curbside eateries was unrestricted. Everything took place out in the open. There was a lot of frenzied action, jumpin' music, a diversity of people, and a minimum number of parents. As an added bonus, the drive-in was a fantastic place to flaunt a car when attempting to make new acquaintances. For those competitive types, it was a handy place to issue race challenges.

Bud Toye, a present-day aficionado of highboy hot rods and owner of The Toye Corporation (a manufacturer of intelligent building systems), still gets a twinkle in his eye when he talks about the drive-in days of his youth: "Very often you would end up with a new date. By the end of the night, the date that you brought with you might have disappeared. People who were not going steady were just cruising around, and sometimes there would be an exchange set up. You didn't always take the same girl home you showed up with! On Monday morning, when you went back to school, you rearranged your social priorities because every

continued on page 56

CRAZY KIDS...
LIVING TO
A WILD
ROCK 'N
ROLL
BEAT!

GENE VINCENT SINGS
"DANCE IN THE STREET" • "BABY BLUE"
"LOVELY LORETTA" • "DANCE TO THE BOP"

HOT ROD GANG

Starring JOHN ASHLEY • JODY FAIR • GENE VINCENT Executive Producer CHARLES BUDDY ROGERS • Produced by LOU RUSOFF • Directed by LEW LANDERS
Story and Screenplay by LOU RUSOFF • A JAMES H. NICHOLSON and SAMUEL Z. ARKOFF PRODUCTION • AN AMERICAN-INTERNATIONAL PICTURE

One of the great fears of the 50s parent was the hot rod gang—crazy kids who lived to a wild rock and roll beat and had no respect for authority or the everyday rules of society. Many thought that the hot rod was a direct conduit to hell and did all they could to stop its proliferation in the streets. ©1958 American International Pictures/Courtesy Mike & Cheryl Goyda

During the 1970s, Increase Records came out with a series of cool nostalgia albums based on the cruisin' and music themes. On each of the nine records (from the cruising golden years of 1955 through 1963), chart toppers from the past rekindled the memories of fun in the streets. Famous disc jockeys from around the country were featured on each of the installments, lending a sense of excitement to the series. Mike Witzel Collection

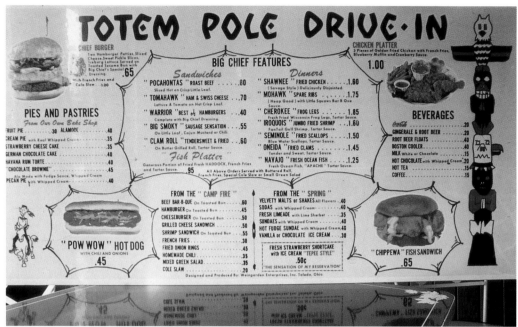

TOTEM POLE DRIVE·IN

CHIEF BURGER .65
Two Hamburger Patties, Sliced Cheese, Sweet Pickle Slices, Iceberg Lettuce Served on Toasted Sesame Bun with Big Chief's Special Dressing.
with French Fries and Cole Slaw 1.00

CHICKEN PLATTER 1.00
2 Pieces of Golden Fried Chicken with French Fries, Blueberry Muffin and Cranberry Sauce.

BIG CHIEF FEATURES

Sandwiches
"POCAHONTAS" ROAST BEEF 80
Sliced Hot on Crisp Little Loaf.
"TOMAHAWK" HAM & SWISS CHEESE . .70
Lettuce & Tomato on Hot Crisp Loaf.
"WARRIOR" "BEST of HAMBURGERS . .40
Complete with Big Chief Dressing.
"BIG SMOKY" SAUSAGE SENSATION . .55
On Little Loaf, Cajun Mustard or Chili.
"CLAM ROLL" TENDERSWEET & FRIED .60
On Butter Grilled Roll, Tartar Sauce.

Fish Platter
Generous Portion of Fried Fresh HADDOCK, French Fries and Tartar Sauce. .95

PIES AND PASTRIES
From Our Own Bake Shop
FRUIT PIE . . . .30 ALAMODE 40
CREAM PIE with Real Whipped Cream . . .35
STRAWBERRY CHEESE CAKE 35
GERMAN CHOCOLATE CAKE 40
HAVANA RUM TORTE 40
"CHOCOLATE BROWNIE" 40
PECAN PIE with Whipped Cream 40
Ala Mode with Fudge Sauce, Whipped Cream .40

Dinners
"SHAWNEE" FRIED CHICKEN 1.60
(Savage Style) Deliciously Disjointed.
"MOHAWK" SPARE RIBS 1.75
(Heap Good) with Little Squaws Bar B Que
"CHEROKEE" FROG LEGS 1.85
Fresh Fried Wisconsin Frog Legs, Tartar Sauce.
"IROQUOIS" JUMBO FRIED SHRIMP .1.60
FanTail Gulf Shrimp, Tartar Sauce.
"SEMINOLE" FRIED SCALLOPS . . .1.50
Blue Water Scallops, Tartar Sauce.
"ONEIDA" FRIED CLAMS 1.45
Tender and Sweet, Tartar Sauce.
"NAVAJO" FRESH OCEAN FISH . . .1.25
Fresh Ocean Fish, "APACHE" Tartar Sauce.
All Above Orders Served with Buttered Roll, French Fries, Special Cole Slaw or Small Green Salad

BEVERAGES
Coca-Cola 20
GINGERALE & ROOT BEER . . .20
ROOT BEER FLOATS 40
BOSTON COOLER 40
MILK White or Chocolate 15
HOT CHOCOLATE with Whipped Cream .20
HOT TEA 15
COFFEE 15

FROM THE "CAMP FIRE"
BEEF BAR-B-QUE On Toasted Bun . . .60
HAMBURGER On Toasted Bun 45
CHEESEBURGER On Toasted Bun . . .50
GRILLED CHEESE SANDWICH 50
SHRIMP SANDWICH On Toasted Bun . .55
FRENCH FRIES 30
FRIED ONION RINGS 45
HOMEMADE CHILI 35
MIXED GREEN SALAD 35
COLE SLAW 20

FROM THE "SPRING"
VELVETY MALTS or SHAKES All Flavors .40
SODAS with Whipped Cream 40
FRESH LIMEADE with Lime Sherbet . .35
SUNDAES with Whipped Cream 40
HOT FUDGE SUNDAE with Whipped Cream.40
VANILLA or CHOCOLATE ICE CREAM . .30

FRESH STRAWBERRY SHORTCAKE
with ICE CREAM "TEEPEE STYLE"
.50¢
"THE SENSATION OF MY RESERVATION"

"CHIPPEWA" FISH SANDWICH .65

"POW WOW" HOT DOG
WITH CHILI AND ONIONS
.45

Designed and Produced By: Weingarden Enterprises, Inc. Toledo, Ohio

---

Located at 1205 South Woodward, the Totem Pole Drive-In was a much-loved fixture along Detroit's Woodward Avenue and anchor of the South end of the strip. Its "Heap Good Food" (and the double-deck burger made of two 1/8-pound patties and flavored with a unique sauce) was once a landmark. Mildred Hund bought the business in 1954 and ran the operation through the cruising years of the fifties, until the lease finally ran out during the seventies. For cruisers, the food and fun had there are now a fond memory. ©1997 Tom Shaw/Musclecar Review Magazine

Continued from page 53

Friday night, you fell in love. Not many relationships survived the weekend!" Without a doubt, the American drive-in restaurant was an important catalyst for making and breaking relationships during the cruisin' heyday.

Unfortunately, the success of the drive-in as a meeting and mating place was one of the main factors that contributed to its decline. By the mid-sixties, kids began parking their hopped-up roadsters and low-slung customs and hanging out all night—jamming the service lanes and barring customers that actually *bought* food. Suddenly, the cacophony of revving engines and rock and roll music became unbearable. By then, the illegal racing was flagrant with races run right out in the open. As the excessive alcohol and drug use inflamed the rage of juvenile delinquents, fights broke out regularly. All across America, lawmakers jumped into action and instituted new rules to regulate the motorized free-for-all.

Unfortunately, the fears of parents and educators were coming true: Dick and Jane had grown up and the car was the instrument of their moral corruption! In 1964, San Bernardino, California, attempted to turn the tide when the city enacted ordinance number 2594. Forced by law, drive-in owners posted the regulation at their eateries with multiple signs. Soon, rambunctious teens found placards with this greeting: "Absolutely no loud or excessive motor noises permitted, operation of the radio at a loud volume level, spinning of wheels, cruising! No loitering, no disorderly conduct, threats, altercations! This will be rigidly enforced by Police Order! Thank You!" For the hooligans who chose to ignore the warnings, the reward was a misdemeanor charge with a hefty $500 fine. In the effort to quell the festivities, some proprietors experimented with a less confrontational approach and used tactics such as controlled-access entry gates, pass-through tokens, and lot patrols.

When drive-in restaurants began replacing carhops with intercom devices such as these, overhead canopies were used to mount the new gadgets. Today, the Sonic drive-in chain uses units like these in addition to human carhops. This classic was found in Eldorado, Kansas. *Mike Witzel*

The drive-in and cruising situation became so inflamed that by 1967 *Drive-In Restaurant* magazine carried "Ordinance Roundup" as a regular feature. That same year, a crowd of 75 to 100 teenagers converged at the McDonald's Drive-In located at Whittier Boulevard in California and took it over. According to the report, they all came, parked, hung out, and made no effort to leave! To counter the teen invasion, manager Arnand Duncan had already been closing the doors on Monday afternoons "to keep the kids from ruining his business." Duncan hired police guards to enforce a no-loitering rule that required patrons to buy their food, eat it, and move out in 20 minutes. The days of cruisers hanging out at Mel's or the Pig Stand while nursing a Coke or malt were over. Cruising would never be the same again.

At drive-ins like this classic programmatic example, street races were planned, and challenges were made—a tailor-made environment for the hot rodder of the 1950s. It was also a great place for custom car builders and hot rodders to hang out and compare notes about how they built their cars, such as the 1957 Chevrolet on the right and the 1950 Mercury (with a chopped top) on the left. *Kent Bash*

The Healthcamp Drive-In is a modern-day drive-in eatery that's a favorite with cruisers in Waco, Texas. A car club that calls itself "The Heart of Texas Street Machines" has adopted the eatery (located on the famous traffic circle) as their favorite destination. Years ago, places like this one defined the points along the many cruising circuits that fanned out on each end of Main. *Mike Witzel*

Out on the streets, the police ticketed the merrymakers who continued to cruise for speeding, street racing, using improper equipment, having too many people stuffed in a car, noisy headers, loitering at businesses, littering, and vandalism. To some, it seemed that the cops dreamed up charges at the spur of the moment. In Detroit, Michigan, a city known for its cars and its cruising, the aimless habit of recreational driving became a serious moving violation that carried point penalties. In 1960, an amendment to the city's official Traffic Ordinance specified "that no automobile operator shall attempt to drive through or upon any driveway in restaurant driveways [sic] or parking lots for purposes other than those for which they were constructed."

Fortunately, there were other places to drive besides Main Street and the service lanes of drive-ins. While the die-hard cruisers were haunting restaurants on the loop, couples were finding their entertainment in places with dimmer lighting. With many of the same characteristics that made the curb service

Woodward Avenue was the Indianapolis for street racers. The legend of this notorious strip began in 1805 when Michigan was still a territory and the internal combustion engine not even a gleam in the eyes of inventors. That year, the entire city was consumed by a stable fire and plans were made to replot the streets. Using the layout of Washington, D.C., as a model, Judge Augustus Woodward was coordinating the rebuilding when he got the idea to rename Detroit's old fur trading route (known as Saginaw Trail) after himself. By the time auto experimenter Charles Brady King drove his primitive motorized horse buggy down the avenue in 1896, the name was one of many that described identical corridors. But this carriage route proved itself to be no ordinary street. By 1928, it had matured into an eight-lane thoroughfare, swelled by the traffic that rolled in and out of Detroit's great car-making machine. ©1997 Tom Shaw/Musclecar Review Magazine

restaurant so immensely popular, the drive-in theater (an outdoor format for viewing movies patented by Richard Milton Hollingshead in 1933) became a secondary destination for the teen on wheels. During the fifties, the admission was affordable and the parking plentiful. Snack bars overflowed with cheap popcorn and soda pop. Unlike the movie houses that occupied a place on Main Street, the audience could watch a movie in complete privacy, choosing to focus their attention on the flickering screen or the person sitting next to them.

After World War II, the number of drive-in theaters boomed from a low of 102 outlets to well over 1,000. By 1949, the drive-in had become the

bastion of the second rate, "B" movie and remained so until the end of its days. No program aired on the tiny television tubes of the period could compare with the larger-than-life epics being projected on the big outdoor screens. Art imitated life in film after film as a barrage of hot rod and juvenile delinquent exploitation titles (featuring fast cars and fast women) exploded onto the scene. When the mania for flying saucers gripped the nation, weird tales of other worlds and aliens grabbed drive-in viewers by the throat and never let go. Science-fiction became all the rage and cruisers flocked to the nearest "ozoner" to watch favorite actor Steve McQueen battle a shapeless

Around midnight, Woodward ripped. It was quitting time for second-shift assembly line workers and a fresh batch of street machines headed for the avenue. Some of these contestants were rogues with bad reputations, while others were just "factory teams" who liked nothing better than mixing it up in the streets. During the day, they walked the halls of corporate America, but at night they prowled Main Street in the name of market research. While these racing forays were unauthorized by the company, street lore has it that John DeLorean and his colleagues regularly cruised the GTO prototype out on Woodward to test it under street conditions. Today, a McDonald's on Woodward pays tribute to those days with a display of classic street machines. *Howard Ande ©1997*

Ray Truelson revived the St. Paul, Minnesota, Porky's in 1990 and made it a haven for classic car owners. The drive-in, walk-up, under-the-canopy- style of service is a favorite for denizens of University Avenue. The California coffee shop–style of restaurant architecture known as "Googie" has helped to make this operation stand out from the fast food banality found at the majority of present-day burger grills. *Michael Dregni*

alien life form in *The Blob*. As teenagers in their cars watched with morbid fascination, the *Devil Girl from Mars* landed and the robot monster *Kronos* trampled everything in its path!

On dates, in groups, alone, or to meet friends, kids cruised out to grand drive-in installations like California's Asuza. To save on the cost of admission, stuffing friends into the trunk became one of the most memorable pastimes. Initially, the ploy worked. Still, the cost-cutting trick was an easy one to spot, as the overloaded trunk caused the rear springs to sink and cars to sit unusually low. Later, a few theaters charged admission to cover a full carload and the practice ended.

By the sixties, though, there were much more serious developments to worry about. Teens were adding hard liquor and drugs like marijuana to their cigarette habit. Adolescents and young adults

Not all Main Street cruisers were hot rods and custom cars. When the 1957 Chrysler 300 came out with its powerful Hemi motor, the automotive pundits lauded it as the fastest production car in America. One of the first muscle cars, it was a motoring machine that lived up to the imposing image of the tail fins adorning its rear end. Equally at ease when it came to going fast and cruising in style, it was a roomy ride suited for long drives to the outskirts of town. *Kent Bash*

indulged themselves in the evil habits of the day and staged impromptu parties in the parking lot of the local drive-in. Of course, the revelry was all in the name of a good cause: hanging out.

By providing a tailor-made arrangement to accommodate the sexual experimentation of adolescents, drive-ins indulged young lovers in the areas that counted: low lighting, free parking, and a lack

In 1957, the drive-in restaurant provided a comfortable place for the American teenager to socialize. There, you could remain in your convertible, partake of tasty foods, and listen to the radio—all while keeping an arm around your favorite girl. Here, Gloria Harper of Oscar Smith High School and all-state fullback Tommy Bland of Maury High School enjoy conversation and curb food at the typical drive-in. *Courtesy Albert Doumar*

61

of adult supervision. For teens with other activities in mind, films were nothing more than mood lighting that provided something to watch while waiting in line at the grill. While owners across the country denied the drive-in's reputation as a "passion pit," people knew that kids with cars were really going there to make out. Try as they might, owners were impotent when it came to controlling what paying customers did in their cars. How could they? Technical matters occupied the projectionist. The ushers were barely adults themselves. At the concession stand, the cooks didn't make enough money to

Anyone who has ever taken a cruise down Route 66 remembers the journey. As a two-lane corridor with a character all its own, a drive down this "great diagonal highway" has always been a trip in itself. For on this two-lane ribbon of asphalt, the ride was often much more important than the destination—especially if the vehicle used to get there was the Chevrolet Corvette. *Mike Witzel/Corvette accessories courtesy Mid America Designs*

The car radio was—and still is—a major part of the cruising scene. Over the AM airwaves, future teenage idols sang of drag-racing, dancing, and romance against a background of electric guitars and pounding drums. From chromed slits in the dashboard, the music of a new generation made its way into the hearts and minds of youthful car culture. As shown by this classic 1946 Ford business coupe, the car radio became an integral part of the dashboard design by the end of the forties and, as a result, a major selling point when the time came to purchase a new vehicle. *Mike Witzel/Ford courtesy Dalton Patterson*

oversee the crowd's conduct. Like it or not, almost everything that the parents feared would happen at the drive-in theater did—including holding hands, nuzzling, cuddling, necking, petting, and yes, sometimes even illicit lovemaking.

In 1956, Dr. Evelyn Duvall acknowledged the existence of these back seat escapades in a school textbook when she wrote that "the automobile had definitely changed courtship." She was right

on the money. As easily as it had become a salon for food and a saloon for drink, young lovebirds transformed the car into a portable bed chamber! Since it was the most accommodating place for cruisers to pull down the sheets, venturing out to the drive-in emerged as yet another rite of passage for America's youth.

By the fifties, the average size of a car seat exceeded the dimensions of the standard sofa. Many had the capability of being removed from the

Located on Victory Boulevard in Van Nuys, California, this popular cruising destination was a veritable movie hot spot during the fifties. Unfortunately, man's obsession with tearing down the vestiges of the past to build anew has rendered this classic example of the outdoor theater extinct. The bulldozer and the wrecking ball were the last attractions that played here, turning a parking lot that was once filled with memories into just another space for a shopping center. ©1997 Mike Wallen

During the 1960s, the remaining drive-in theaters still scattered across the United States were managing to hold their own. Although attendance was dropping every year, it would take another decade before the boom in outdoor entertainment became a total bust. By the end of the eighties, watching a movie in a car was no longer a favorite pastime for most motorists. *Courtesy American Automobile Manufacturers Association*

The 1952 Studebaker provided the occupants of the front seat and the back seat ample room to pursue the types of nocturnal cruising activities that were defining the emerging American car culture of the fifties. *Courtesy of the Automotive Hall of Fame*

The Van Nuys Drive-In Theater used to be the primary destination for teenagers who desired a movie and some privacy. Back in the fifties, it was *the* place for entertainment in the California city of Van Nuys, and it remained so for decades. Sadly, this portrait of a 1940 Ford Deluxe Coupe remains as only a reminder of the site; the ozoner was bulldozed a few years ago and part of the area's cruising heritage was lost forever. *Kent Bash*

car completely! Whenever the urge struck, lovers unlatched the seats and laid them out to provide a ready-made bed for "camping." Perhaps the most dramatic example of convertible comfort was the big boat introduced by Nash in 1949. Marketed to families who took highway vacations, its twin fold-down seating arrangement transformed the beast into a rolling boudoir! Custom-built for couples eager to trip the light fantastic, it was one car that parents rarely loaned to children—especially if they planned on cruising. "I knew exactly what was going on at the drive-in," recalls Mrs. A. C. Stewart, a former ticket-taker and usher, now a great-grandmother. "I saw firsthand the goings-on. My kids were never allowed to go without a suitable chaperone . . ."

Fortunately, the love-struck cruisers who overstepped the boundaries of decency at the drive-in theater had other options for parking. There were more secluded locations to consider, including the "submarine races" held out at the lake and the many places called Lover's Lane, Mulholland Drive, or the Point. In the back seat of a car, many a lad or lass found their thrill up on the same "Blueberry Hill" that Fats Domino was singing about. It was all part of the cruising agenda: Once a girl or guy became a willing passenger, trying to get them out to a romantic roadside hideaway later in the evening was all part of the game. When both of the partners agreed, it was off to join other lovebirds at the local make-out spots (usually on the outskirts of town where the view was good—as if anyone wanted to take in the "view" through the

steamed-up windows). Still, despite all entreaties, it didn't always work out for some. Guys who struck out with their companions and didn't take "no" for an answer resorted to using the oldest tricks in the book: engine trouble or running out of gas.

Cruisers who wished to take their girls parking across state boundaries had to resist this temptation. There was one good reason: The Mann Act, a law originated in 1910 as the "White Slave Traffic Act," called for penalties to be levied against any person who knowingly persuaded (or even caused to be persuaded) any girl under age 18 from any state to any other state, with the intent that she be induced to engage in "debauchery." Cruisers who took dates to juke joints out of state (and were stupid enough to have sex with them against their will) faced harsh felony charges, along with a fine of up to $10,000, and a term of imprisonment not exceeding five years!

Despite a plethora of ordinances and denouncements, many of the nation's cruisers took the new rules in stride and openly defied the will of the establishment. The urge to drive free and unfettered was just too strong to resist. Kids were hard-wired to the automobile and had gasoline in their blood. Cruising was their favorite form of automotive recreation and an activity that no one with a car could ignore or deny.

By the time that duck-walking guitar man Chuck Berry released the tune *No Particular Place to Go* in 1964, the countless feeder roads and lesser-traveled traffic spurs that defined the nation's growing motorways joined Main Street and, suddenly, cruising occurred just about everywhere. Sure, the ride had no real destination, but who gave a hoot? Teenagers were discovering for themselves the wonders of the automobile and were feeling absolutely no shame about "cruisin' and playin' the radio," even if they just drove around in circles and had "no particular place to go!"

CHICKEN-RACE!
ROCK 'N ROLL!
YOUTH ON THE LOOSE!

Teen-age Terrorists burning up the streets!

HOT-ROD GIRL

Addicted to Speed and Horsepower

When the Cruisers Craved Street Racing

"My first car was a 1937 Ford sedan that I picked up in 1959 for the modest payout of 40 bucks. Even though it wasn't any kind of a record breaker in the speed department, it ran great. My second was a 1938 Buick coupe with a straight-eight engine that I bought for $50. By that time, I was an experienced cruiser and was ready for some get-up-and-go. So I pulled the tired straight-eight engine that came stock and dropped in a Cadillac flathead! Even though the '48 motor was a lot heavier, it more than made up for its weight difference with the extra power it turned out.

A fenderless 1934 Ford arrives on the scene with a stereotypical cruiser of the fifties era (complete with ducktail 'doo and white T-shirt) at the wheel. The primer gray vehicle is a 1937 Willys sedan, and the yellow machine a 1940 Ford Deluxe Coupe. Looks like a challenge to race will soon be issued here, something that occurred often at the drive-in diner. *Kent Bash*

That was good, because most of the kids that I went to school with were addicted to cars, hot rods, and going fast. Back then, we didn't have video games to play and we didn't spend hours staring at a computer screen. We got our kicks by getting our hands dirty with motor oil, gasoline, and all the other stuff that keeps a car going. Cars were part of our personality, and to us, they meant everything. When we weren't in class, we were out in the streets checking out other fast cars to see what guys were doing to make them run better and figuring out how we could do the same. We spent a lot of time scrounging around the local junkyards looking for small-block Chevy motors and other car parts.

With all of the speed equipment that was becoming available, the small-block Chevy could be refitted with a three-two manifold or even an Iskenderian cam. If you had access to a small machine shop, you could mill the heads to pick up more compression. After just a few basic changes, you could drop one of these "mills" into a vintage Model A chassis and have yourself a pretty hot car. For the guys I cruised the strip with, nothing was more bitchin' than owning a light-weight car with a big eight-cylinder engine, flames painted on the sides of the hood, a stick shift topped off with a small piston head or a menacing skull knob, and cool wheels!

Unfortunately, when muscle cars began showing up at the many cruising circuits of the sixties, the scene began to change. Any guy who could afford to buy himself a new or used one had himself a powerful street machine right off the dealer's parking lot.

By the seventies, it didn't take a lot of imagination or tinkering to build a cool street rod and, of course, the hard-core hot rodder resented this. Now, almost anybody without car know-how could slap down a few bucks for a fast car, challenge you to a race the next day, and beat your pants off. Yeah, there were lots of crazy drivers and lots of smashed muscle cars. Gearheads like us hung out at the wrecking yards just so we could get the first crack at salvaging the motors and trannys to put into our own hot rods!"

—*Kent Bash*

Chapter Three

FOR teenage lads of the forties and fifties, building a hot rod was just about the most counterculture activity one could indulge in—short of robbing gas stations and purse-snatching. When cocooned by the chrome and steel armor of a hot rod, young boys could amplify their personality and improve upon their identity. While driving a souped-up car, the average adolescent assumed an attitude—bashful boys became braver, and careful kids turned careless. Even the meek, mild-mannered Clark Kent types got a chance to play four-wheeled Superman. All it took to gain possession of these strange new powers was to own a powerful heap. All the better if it was fast and could win a few races.

During the hop-up heyday that defined the postwar era, the hot rod became a metaphor for the sexual prowess of the American male and the race a means to prove it. Rambunctious hot rodders who were eager to make a name for themselves challenged others who were driving similar cars to meet them, and then try to beat them. Although street racing had been around since the days of the first horseless carriages, never before were the conditions so right for illegal, one-on-one racing in the streets. Gas was cheap and used cars (that provided fodder for race rods) were affordable. Leisure time was abundant. Impressionable motorheads avoided street gangs (other than car clubs), and when violent clashes took place, seldom were Saturday night specials used to settle

California's Foothill Boulevard, better known as Route 66, was a microcosm of the cruising ideal during the mid-1950s. Everything one could think of that smacks of nostalgia could be found along this stretch of street, including automotive dealerships, drive-in restaurants, coffee shops, and more. Along this well-traveled route, the car was king. At intersections like this one, racing challenges were issued around the clock. ©1997 Dave Wallen

them. Rodders raised in the back seat and weaned on high-octane fuel were more creative: Racing slicks, tuned headers, and a floor-mounted stick shift were the cruiser's dueling weapons. The smooth pavement of the public streets was the preferred place to shoot it out.

Unofficially, the two-lane tango of cruising began during the impetuous years of the Roaring Twenties. While careful car owners stayed within the posted limits, a small clique of wealthy car enthusiasts got the idea to drive their Duesenbergs out to the dry lake beds north of Los Angeles, California, just to see how fast they could go. Ostracized from everyday corridors of travel, these

Honk magazine was one of the first publications to specialize in the car—the way young guys liked them. Profuse mechanical and construction details were a hallmark of the magazine and aided many a rodder in building a hot ride. *Courtesy Mike & Cheryl Goyda*

early pioneers of speed realized that locations like Muroc Dry Lake offered acres of the unobstructed space they needed to test the limits of high-speed cruising, without fear of being thrown in jail by the local constable. Without admission charges and no one to monitor them, a single standard emerged: no rules! Four-wheeled adventurers who liked to take their cars to the outer edge and beyond were left to their own devices.

While affluent car jockeys attempted to do things that no one else even dared doing with their cars, so-called normal automobile owners observed from the sidelines in awe, never suspecting that someday their kids would try similar feats out in the streets. But as the years passed, the unexpected did happen: The high-speed dance with death turned from an occasional oddity into a regular hobby. Cars were becoming affordable, and soon it was the Model T that saw lake bed action. The interest became intense. By the mid-thirties, dry lake beds became the premiere place for organized speed trials for the everyman.

"Tinkering with race cars and dinking around with motors was a kick back in those days," recalled Halvin "the Jackrabbit" Releg, a retired, one-time dry lakes racer and speed equipment salesman (who claims welding frames for various rods took up 20 years of his life). "When I was a senior [in high school], I burned up most of my extra time working on hot rods, building them up from junk

HONK!

CUSTOM CARS • HOT RODS

WHY a HOT IGNITION?
By Ak Miller

MAY 1953
25c

• SPARKLING CUSTOMS • UNIQUE HOT RODS
• MECHANICAL and CONSTRUCTION DETAILS

After the rusting wrecks of $10 cars were dragged from the junk heaps back to suburbia, the driveway became the hot rodder's domain for repair work. The vehicle receiving a close inspection in this scene is a 1932 roadster; to the left is a 1934 Ford Phaeton, and on the street sits a Model A sedan of 1928 vintage. For some unlucky parents, scenes like this were a never-ending nightmare of spilled oil, rusted parts, and uncompleted car projects. Not all hot rod wannabees were as industrious as this crew. *Kent Bash*

scrap and stuff and figurin' out how to fit the pieces and parts together. Heck, my pals and I took every chance we could to cruise our cars to the flats to run 'em. Going fast was almost better than sex! We loved speed and had no problem gettin' our jollies without drugs!"

In those fledgling days of dry lakes racing, the top speed of a car determined its standing among other contestants. As a result, clocking, or timing a racer's rate of travel between marked points became the defining activity. In a heat known as a "match run," cars lined up with similar machines to race. But that's where the similarities ended: Unlike the lap races held at oval tracks, vehicles sped across the cracked mud in a straight line without turning. After accelerating to a rolling start, the one vehicle that made the fastest elapsed time between measuring posts became the winner. Spectators and participants loved all the action, even though it was a loud, dirty, and highly dangerous pastime.

To the mixed reactions of participants, a group called the Southern California Timing Association (SCTA) organized in 1937. All of a sudden, rules and regulations began encroaching on the once open and carefree contests! Timed match runs were no more and classes grouped cars according to their type. In an effort to nix the dust created when multiple vehicles ran, new guidelines specified that only two cars at a time could compete against one another. While they waited to make their run, a few participants took inspiration from the fresh format and began to stage their own heats. There were a few minor

Oval track racing was very popular in the forties and fifties. While some hopped-up cars were built for the street and others for the drags, track racers liked nothing better than wheeling around a dirt circle in pursuit of the checkered flag. Shown here is a 1933 Ford three-window coupe with a flathead engine. *Courtesy John White*

changes in the way the heat runs were operated versus top-speed runs. The timing aspect wasn't so important, even though races ran in a straight line. Instead of a rolling start, cars took off from a standstill. Now, whoever crossed the finish line first claimed the win. Because the main technique

The pre-1937 Jalopies that were raced on oval tracks were usually stripped of their soft tops, lending an odd look to the event. When racing at night, it wasn't uncommon to catch glare from the lights and be distracted from the action. What happened next was something the spectators knew could happen at any given moment: accidents, wrecks, and rollovers. Along with winning, it was all part of the show. *Courtesy John White*

Bob Johnson and Rueben Thrash raced jalopies at the Veterans Stadium in Long Beach, California, during the mid-fifties. In stark contrast to the big-money racing events that are held today, it was a "kinder and gentler" time. Back then, the cars were simple, the tracks were made of dirt, people were friendly, and competition was largely just for the fun of it. *Courtesy John White*

Ironically, the cruisers that regularly caroused the commercial passageway called Main (like this Fort Worth, Texas, strip) seldom stopped anywhere along its length to conduct business. For those motoring around in menacing hot rods and cool customs, remaining static for too long was a practice tantamount to heresy. Almost always, a street machine that was at rest resulted in its driver being made to shell out more money, answer to a higher authority, explain intentions, or heed lectures on how to behave. In the long run, it was less confrontational to remain in motion and to slow the car only when hangouts that catered to young people were passed. *Mike Witzel*

for victory was to gain quick acceleration by dragging in low gear as long as possible, the event became known as a "drag race."

Jazzed by the uninhibited aura of drag racing, West Coast car fanatics who called themselves "hop-up" artists began flocking to Muroc and El Mirage dry lakes to "run what you brung." Often, the enthusiasm waned when the occasional weekend racer realized that the blowing dust, glaring sun, and baking 100-

By the end of World War II, half of America's 26 million automobiles were 10 years old. To meet the rising demand for new vehicles, the Detroit automotive machine churned out new models, producing as many cars in the span of five years that had been plying the roadways before the war. Suddenly, used cars were available everywhere. The surplus of vehicles became the prime stock for hot rodders and customizers to express their art. Here, a maroon 1932 Ford roadster, a blue 1936 Ford three-window coupe, and a 1937 Chevy are on display. Later, when muscle cars roared out of the factories, dealers like this one sold ready-made street machines to a willing market. *Kent Bash*

Speed shops became the primary location for hot rodders to buy the parts and equipment needed to hop up their rides. Some of the early suppliers of specialty parts started in the teens and the business blossomed into a major industry by the 1950s. Today, speed parts are everywhere and even the car parts outfit down at the local strip mall carries a certain amount of custom wheels and other accessories that at one time would have been regarded as specialty items. *Mike Witzel*

degree temperatures weren't always conducive to a fun time. While dyed-in-the-wool time trial participants and their entourages had no problem enduring the conditions, the spectators had a hard go of it. By that time, the drag racing sideshow was splintering off into its own unique category. For the complete expression of the quirky new sport, locations that were better suited to hold races and boosters of the growing racing hobby began looking elsewhere.

The timing was just right, since a smattering of ready-made racing strips in the southern

When the craze for hot rodding was at its peak during the fifties, club jackets and T shirts emblazoned with the name of one's car club were extremely popular garb. At a glance, car nuts could identify their competitors at the track, while giving each individual a sense of group membership and camaraderie. Today, these items of attire are hot collectibles. *Mike Witzel/jackets courtesy Mike and Cheryl Goyda*

California area were just waiting for reclamation. Faster than you could fill a gas tank and clip the nozzle back onto the pump, the abandoned aircraft runways left over after World War II became the new locations for drag racing competition. Behind Newport Bay in the city of Santa Ana, C. J. Hart discovered a quiet little airfield and turned it into one of drag racing's classic venues. Offering

10 percent of the take right off the top, he struck a deal with the airport's manager to rent out one of the unused runways every Sunday morning. The track opened in the fall of 1950 and the sounds of drag racing reverberated across the tarmac—drowning out the propellers of the little planes taxiing nearby. Soon, quarter-mile racing strips that featured specially built facilities appeared in

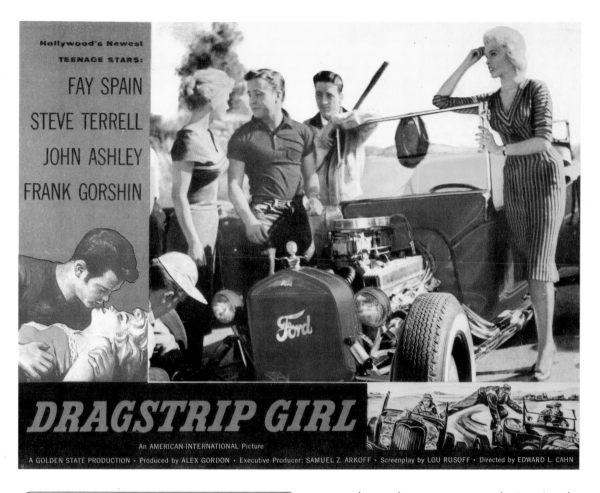

Hollywood's Newest
TEENAGE STARS:

FAY SPAIN

STEVE TERRELL

JOHN ASHLEY

FRANK GORSHIN

DRAGSTRIP GIRL

An AMERICAN-INTERNATIONAL Picture

A GOLDEN STATE PRODUCTION · Produced by ALEX GORDON · Executive Producer: SAMUEL Z. ARKOFF · Screenplay by LOU RUSOFF · Directed by EDWARD L. CAHN

©1957 American International Pictures/Courtesy Ron Main

places like Pamona and Fontana and from there, opened across America.

Even so, hot rodders faced growing opposition from the establishment. Alarmed by the growing amount of street racing, police organizations and the popular press began working the media propaganda machine in hopes of turning public sentiment against the hot rodders. It was the distinct wish of the powers-that-be to ban all hot rods from the roadways.

Concerned about the tide of opposition that was rising against the hot rod hobby, Wally Parks, then the general manager of the Southern California Timing Association, joined forces with Robert E. Petersen of Hollywood Publicity Associates. Together, they had a brainstorm to

stage a hot rod extravaganza at the Los Angeles Armory that would show Joe Public that the average hot rodder was much more than a lawbreaking juvenile delinquent. Some big name Hollywood stars were recruited to attend the pair's souped-up soiree, and as a direct consequence a respectable number of radio, television, and newspaper reporters followed.

However, it was the hot rodders and their gleaming creations that ultimately stole the limelight from the Tinsel Town celebrities. By providing potent examples of ingenious automotive engineering, unlimited creativity, and endless imagination, they managed to make the promotional gala a resounding success. The proof was more than just a few superficial accolades printed in the papers. After the event, even the National Safety Council abandoned its negative attitude towards hot rodding. As hard as it was to believe, the

A gleaming black, flamed fenderless Ford with "big n' little" tires, a blacked-out radiator grille, and fully chromed engine (complete with a blower) strikes a rather sinister-looking pose at a favorite car gathering in Augusta, Kansas. Just looking fast was an important asset to all street racers. *Mike Witzel*

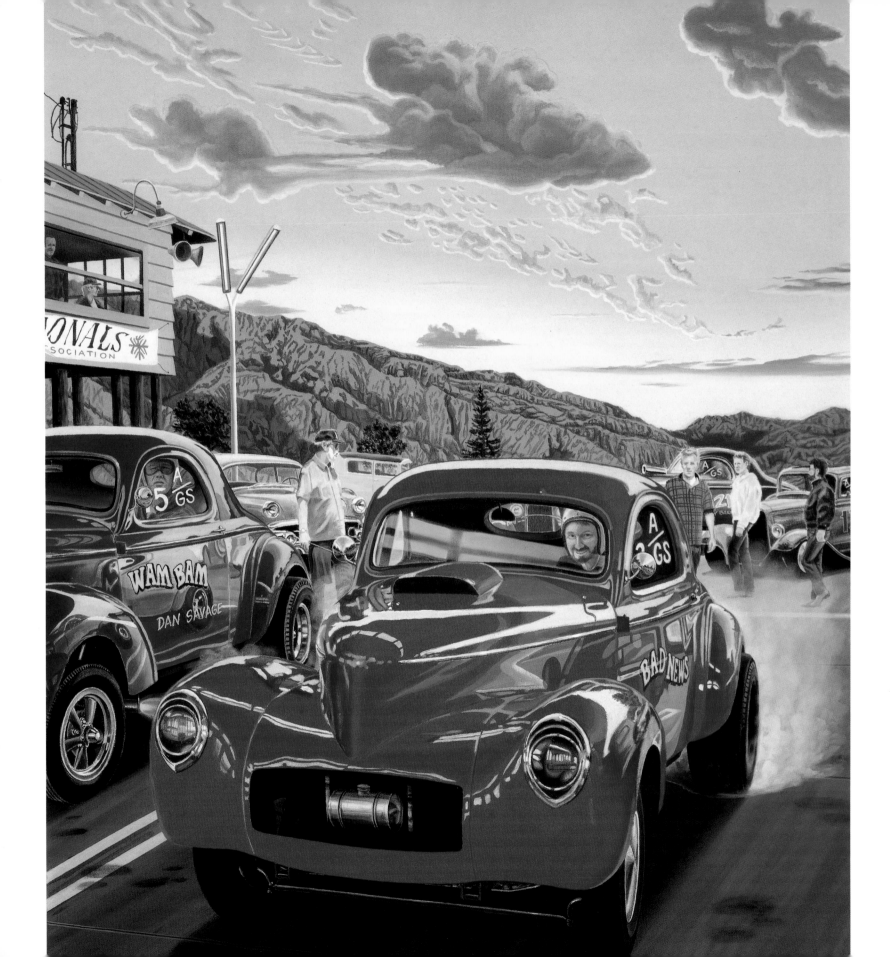

Southern California Timing Association was asked to become a member! Supercharged by the development and the groundswell of acceptance that followed, Petersen went on to produce *Hot Rod* magazine with Parks joining as the publication's editor in 1948.

But that was only the beginning of respectability for the hot rod realm. In 1951, The National Hot Rod Association was formed under the leadership of Wally Parks and went on to promote and popularize drag racing nationwide. Under the aegis of the NHRA, a promotional caravan called the Safety Safari (with a full Chrondek timing outfit) toured the country to recruit new racers and fans. In addition to introducing a new generation to the many wonders of the hot rod, this portable drag strip showed police that hot rodders were aware—and concerned—about safety.

Structured hot rod events gained respect and it wasn't long before the general public had drag racing rituals like the National Championships and the Winternationals to attend every year. By 1956, the sport boasted over 130 legal drag racing strips in the United States with more than 100,000 hot rods reported to be cruising the highways and byways. That year, a staggering 2.5 million spectators turned out to watch the drags! With the 1956 speed record set at 166 miles per hour, the public interest in this former fringe activity was electrified. Meanwhile, former illegal street racers were lured to the sport, and hot rod clubs around the nation claimed that they were signing up some 1,500 new members each month!

Speeding off towards the future, drag racing was destined to go totally "commercial." Soon, specialized dragsters, or "rail jobs" that looked nothing like the vehicles that had pioneered the sport appeared at the strips. In place of brakes, remote-release parachutes assumed the job of slowing a racer's considerable momentum. Engines swelled in size and began sucking in exotic mixtures of explosive fuels. Rear wheels fattened as front tires took a cue from the bicycle. In the end, it was no longer a man driving the machine—the machine drove the man.

Attracted more to the smell of money than the strong odor of race fuel, corporate America caught wind of the phenomenon, and before too long big money flooded into drag racing. Within a few brief years, the inevitable sponsorships and commercialism that followed completely changed the racing scene. By the time America had accomplished its first manned exploration of the moon, the only unregulated, spur-of-the-moment hot rod activities that remained were taking place on the asphalt of America's streets.

Despite advances made in civilizing the hot rod animal, unsanctioned speed runs enjoyed by cruisers remained a disturbing reality—even in the cities that were lucky enough to have lawful racing

This one-time gasser has been made over into an attention-getting street rod. Here, it's parked at the Canoga Park Bob's Big Boy Cruise Night prior to closing. Now, this former drive-in dining location has been converted into just another chain restaurant. While cruise nights and carousing are over, the cruisers are still allowed to visit. *Kent Bash*

The 1932 Ford three-window coupe in the fenderless highboy configuration was—and still is—an extremely popular style of hot rod. Like the custom coach builders of motoring's early years, the teenagers growing up in automotive America developed tricks and techniques that rivaled the expertise of the finest craftsmen. The chopped top, as exemplified in this whimsical scene, became one of the more prominent modifications. First used by the dry lakebed racers to decrease air resistance, it was retained for its cool visual effect when the racing activities moved onto the streets. The car in this scene is a real-life model owned by famed car culture artist Robert Williams. *Kent Bash*

In its day, the Greer, Black, and Prudhomme Top Fuel was the most winning dragster in the history of drag racing. As indicated by this classic machine, dragster engines were first positioned in front of the drivers. After racer Don Garlits nearly blew his foot off in a racing disaster, he was the first to build a successful dragster with the engine positioned behind the driver. Others saw the logic and followed suit until it became a standard.*Courtesy Gary Lick*

...IT'S WHERE THE BOYS MEET THE GIRLS...and everyone can SEE what they're gonna be up against!

SEE THE BEACH-PARTY GANG GO DRAGSTRIP!

AMERICAN INTERNATIONAL presents IN PANAVISION® AND PATHÉCOLOR

Bikini Beach

STARRING

FRANKIE AVALON • "ANNETTE" FUNICELLO • MARTHA HYER • HARVEY LEMBECK • DON RICKLES • JOHN ASHLEY • JODY McCREA

CANDY JOHNSON • LITTLE STEVIE WONDER • THE PYRAMIDS | SPECIAL GUEST STAR KEENAN WYNN | Directed by WILLIAM ASHER • Produced by JAMES H. NICHOLSON and SAMUEL Z. ARKOFF

Written by WILLIAM ASHER & LEO TOWNSEND and ROBERT DILLON

outlets. In 1947, the movie *Devil On Wheels* had brought a new awareness of the speed problem to God-fearing citizens: In the film, a young boy named Mickey slaps together his first hot rod, and then uses it to make racing challenges out along the back roads. Without a doubt, impressionable teens in the audience were eager to jump in their own machines and give 'er the gun. "Problem was, everybody wanted to go fast in a souped hot rod," lamented amateur drag racer Hervez Zapata. "We dug the racing thing so much that we couldn't always hold out for the

drag strip to open up. Besides, most of the dudes with bad cars wanted to show them off where other people—I guess girls—could see them do crazy stuff. Taking a rod way out to race them legally in the boonies wasn't always first choice. The street was real fun!" To the chagrin of society's rulemakers, the nation's hot rodding subculture became so inebriated with cars and competition that they had to find places to race—even when the legal strips closed!

As a rather unfortunate side effect of the lack of large numbers of drag strips, cruisers embraced

©1964 American International Pictures/Courtesy Ron Main

CLASS TROPHY

Champion

MINNESOTA DRAGWAYS

INTERNATIONAL

IHRA

HOT ROD ASSOCIATION

NHRA

springnationals

1969 DALLAS

NEW YORK

ELIMINATOR

NATIONAL SPEEDWAY

RACEWAY PARK

CLASS WINNER
ENGLISHTOWN, N.J.

RACEWAY PARK

NHRA

SANCTIONED STRIP

CLASS WINNER

UNITED STATES
GAS AND FUEL
CHAMPIONSHIP DRAGS

BAKERSFIELD—SMOKERS

1967

LIONS DRAG STRIP

NG BEACH, CALIF. CLASS WINNER

floor

HURST

shift

CECIL COUNTY DRAGWAY

CLASS CHAMPION

NATIONAL WINNER SPEEDWAY

NEW YORK CITY'S
CONNECTING HIGHW

POLICE

DEDICATED TO SPEED

STREET RACE WINNER

5th ANNUAL

WORLD FINALS

NHR

AMERICAN
HOT ROD ASSOCIATION

AHRA

CLASS WINNER

Atco

DRAGWAY

PITTSBURGH INTERNATIONAL

DRAGWAY

LASS CHAMPIO

1969

the paved thoroughfares that poured out all across America and made them the destination for recreational racing. There was good reason, since the conditions in the streets were optimal. There weren't any major bumps to contend with, rocks to dodge, or big obstacles to endanger the path of reckless drivers (if one didn't count all of the other cars). For the hot rod rowdy who liked nothing better than seeing how fast his car could go, the message was clear: Not only were these improved roads and highways great locations to go cruising, they were also perfect racing venues. Who cared if it was an illegal activity?

After sundown, secluded hideaways became impromptu meeting places where many of the car clubs conducted illegal drag racing. Not surprisingly, cruisers in California were the most imaginative, and locations like the concrete drainage basin of the Los Angeles River became top spots for clandestine hot rod action. There were hundreds of others prized by the growing street mob, including the smooth roads without cross-traffic like Sepulveda Boulevard. The remote cut of asphalt that ran by the Van Norman Dam and reservoir was a big draw, as was the ribbon of Foothill Boulevard (Route 66) that unfurled past the Santa Anita horse track in Arcadia. Mines Field (an airstrip that later became Los Angeles International Airport) brought to mind a favorite nearby strip called Lincoln Boulevard. Close by in El Monte, illegal racing scarred Peck Road. Still, the best run of all was over in Burbank. Just west of the city limits, Glen Oaks Boulevard boasted an ideal location: Burbank cops didn't have authority across the city boundary, and the Los Angeles squad cars had to come out all the way from the Van Nuys substation!

But whether it was a public traffic strip on the East Coast, a secluded back road on the West Coast, or any of myriad roadways in between, the story was pretty much the same: Street race riffraff wanted nothing to do with civility. This was a style without established guidelines where participants made up the protocol as they went. Hot rod heathens cruising the strip scoffed at traffic laws, snickered at speed limits, and thumbed their noses at authority. A large part of the illegal street racing mystique was disregarding (and breaking) normal traffic laws. "Engaging in a speed contest" became the phrase most feared by street racers, and police regularly chased down the daredevils to issue them a ticket.

Sometimes, things got serious with real bullets fired! At a "cruise night" held in 1996 in New England, an outspoken New Yorker (who preferred to remain anonymous) described a frightening incident that forever changed his outlook on unlawful cruising. "Uh, huh, we took some lead once and let me tell 'ya, it wasn't fun. It all started when we was dragging our favorite strip under this

Cruising the strip was never an unregulated activity. Police patrols were always on hand to keep street racers in check and limit the activities of overexuberant youth. With the widespread addition of the two-way transceiver during the fifties, keeping in touch with nearby squad cars (and central dispatch) made it easy for the boys in blue to nab teenage speeders and other lawbreakers. *From the collections of the Texas/Dallas History and Archives Division, Dallas Public Library*

Model Marrlyn Kwast cradles the carb that furnished fuel for the "one-lung," 7-horsepower engine mounted in the Olds curved dash runabout, produced from 1900 to 1905. Shown below is the 1957 Oldsmobile J-2 "Rocket Engine." With three dual carburetors that provided some 300 horsepower, power-packed motors like this one became the basis for the hot rodding hobby and the reason speeds kept rising. *The Automotive Hall of Fame*

freeway overpass out on Long Island and got busted by the cops. My buddy and I already had 16 tickets between us so we made a run for it in my T. Rounding a turn to ditch 'em on some side streets that we knew by heart, we heard a few slugs whiz by us and we almost wet our pants. Later, we found one of 'em stuck in the turtle!"

Guns were only one deterrent to the street racers. Alarmed by the growing popularity of the illicit "sport," both the police and popular press worked to turn public sentiment against the sort of delinquents who liked to race. As early as the mid-forties, the National Safety Council teamed up with the Hearst Newspaper chain to implement a publicity campaign calling for a ban on automotive racing—both in the streets *and* on the track.

More trouble came in 1945 when California lawmakers introduced Assembly Bill No. 408. Simply put, the statute demanded that "every motor vehicle shall be equipped with four fenders and mudguards." Among rodders who liked to cut the wheel shields off their heaps, the news was unwelcome. Bill 910 followed suit with more dictatorial, if not unconstitutional, words: "No equipment shall be installed upon a motor when it is used to propel a motor vehicle, which is designed to increase the horsepower of the motor above that which it had at the time it was manufactured." Translation: no hopped up engines!

In practice, not one of these actions created the roadblock that was necessary to bar the shortcut to hell's highway. The hot rod race had become a part of America's streets, and the government agencies were impotent when it came to capping the craze. The only recourse was to deal with the problem on a family level. And so, Mama, Papa, Grandma, and Grandpa all attempted to warn Junior of the dangers of driving an overpowered, underbraked street machine with reckless abandon. Of course, the warnings fell on deaf ears. As had been the case since the beginning of the automotive age, teenagers with cars imagined that they were invincible and immune to hazards. Street-racing addicts didn't want to hear of the risks and thought it better to blindly follow the muse of speed, often with dire consequences.

Sadly, this was one time when the old fogies of America were dead right. In the hands of the inexperienced driver, a fast car was like a stick of dynamite with a short fuse. With just a little spark, it could blow up in your face and wrap itself around a telephone pole or roll topsy-turvy through a roadside ditch. That's exactly what happened in one of the most famous hot rod mishaps of the thirties. As the story goes, Phil Weiand (a noted designer and manufacturer of automotive speed equipment) was driving his hopped-up Model T Ford with a friend. He was driving at a rather high speed when he encountered a sharp curve and decided to go for it. Despite Weiand's

Mopar muscle car enthusiasts loved the Max Wedge powerplant, and in 1964, Dodge cars that came equipped with the powerful engine were hands-down favorites for all kinds of racing. *Kent Bash*

The 1965 Chevy Chevelle was a muscle car favorite of the sixties. Chevy made the 396 an option late that year and turned the model into a powerful street contender. *Mike Witzel*

In 1964, John DeLorean and Pontiac engineers slapped a 389-cubic-inch V-8 powerhouse under the hood of a Tempest, stiffened the suspension, and added heavy-duty brakes. He borrowed the Ferrari designation Gran Turismo Omologato and used the first three letters of the strange-sounding handle to add a sense of mystique to his new marque: GTO. By 1966, the model was refined even further and emerged as one of the most remembered muscle machines of all time. *The American Automobile Manufacturers Association*

confidence, his pal in the passenger seat had doubts about the successful execution of the turn. He panicked, yanking the parking brake handle in reaction. Tragically, the roadster flipped out of control with both occupants thrown out. The accident left Weiand a paraplegic.

Competitive driving left many cars incapacitated as well, as a penchant for street racing resulted in a lot of expensive wear and tear on a vehicle's mechanical components. If a rookie driver applied too much power at the wrong time or shifted incorrectly, the excessive rpm could blow an engine.

With its race-bred pedigree, the 426 Hemi threw considerable excitement into the muscle car arena when it was unleashed on the street in 1964 (it was immediately banned from racing). To get the Hemi homologated for NASCAR, Dodge had to make the engine a regular production option for its regular vehicle line-up. Before long, it could be found in such normally staid cars as the 1966 Plymouth Satellite shown here. However, it reached its full potential when it powered muscle cars like the Dodge Charger and Plymouth Roadrunner. *Kent Bash*

Jackrabbit starts ragged out the clutch or tranny and quick stops burned up brakes. Tires were another major casualty of fast cruising, burning rubber, and hard cornering. Van Nuys, California, auto shop teacher David Rodarte recalled the mechanical failures. During the sixties, he discovered the meaning of being stranded when he blew out the driveshaft on his 1965 Galaxy. "I hit third gear at about 110 miles per hour . . . twisted off the output shaft, rolled it up a hill and then down into my friend's front yard! He lived in the projects, so I paid his little brother to sleep in the car while I walked home to get a truck so I could tow it back. As a matter of fact, it's one of the pieces I show off to my auto shop students—that old output shaft all twisted off from the four-speed, with the driveshaft yoke still attached to it!"

Since street racing could commence at the spur of the moment, challengers had the most luck if they maintained their vehicles in top condition. In the days of tail fins and two-tone, all it took to arrange a racing heat was a chance encounter of

In 1967, Dodge rolled out a reconfigured version of the Coronet. It dubbed the revamped street racer the Charger and equipped it with four bucket seats, a full-length center console, and a complete set of dashboard gauges. Although its external characteristics looked somewhat peculiar, a lot of cars got clipped by it on the quarter mile: Mopar fans could order a powerful 426 Hemi installed at the factory. *Courtesy Wes Pieper*

two hot cars at a traffic signal, stop sign, or country crossroads. After both drivers eyeballed each other's car, a deadpan nod signaled that the race was on. From there, two complete strangers with nothing in common but four tires and a modified motor entered into a game that allowed only one winner.

This archetype of racing in the public traffic corridors came to life in the seventies motion picture *American Graffiti*. In one of the more memorable scenes, the local street champ slips along Main Street in a yellow deuce coupe when he's confronted by a stranger piloting a sinister black, hopped-up 1955

The Chevrolet Corvette began its life as an underpowered "sporty" car. In later years, it emerged as a powerful, full-blown muscle machine. Cruisers who could afford one made the Vette the king of all street machines, and on Main Street it ruled. *Courtesy American Automobile Manufacturers Association*

Chevrolet. Of course, the local hero agrees to take on the out-of-town invader, and the pair meet at an illegal drag racing location on the edge of town. As Wolfman Jack howls on the radio in the background, they roar into the dawn and discover that the old master's rod ain't as fast as it used to be. In a twist of fate, the Chevy flips over and crashes, allowing the local paladin to hold his title—for the moment. As was true on the legal strips, someone faster was always waiting on the sidelines to speed by and grab your crown.

For the street racers who wanted more than a quick pickup, the local drive-in restaurant became the place to camp out with your hot rod. By the end of the fifties, numerous car clubs and lone-wolf cruisers had transformed America's hamburger stands into street racing staging areas. No longer was the drive-in serving stall used to eat food! Much to the concern of owners trying to make a buck, curb stands became a great place for youths to park a hot rod, display it, and tinker with the engine while waiting for the next challenger to

come along. While one munched on an order of french fries or sucked down a milkshake, it was easy to arrange illegal match-ups for later in the evening. Eventually, the drive-in scene became so crazy that some participants towed their hot rods out on trailers and parked them across the street! For these guys, drag racing was serious business. All of the time and money used to tune and trick out a car demanded a reward with some sort of prize—namely, tangible personal property.

At the time, the legal drag racing strips of the day often awarded little trophies to the winners. With that fact in mind, street racers wanted their bonus as well. Many racers who already had a number of notches carved in their belt became bored with the simple contest of one-upmanship and began looking for new ways to raise the thrill level. To increase the risk and heighten fun, they staged a fair amount of "boulevard brawling" to win material possessions like cigarettes, leather jackets,

Two muscle cars, Dodge and Pontiac, face off against each other out in the streets of Detroit. During the 1970s, confrontations like this one were a nightly occurrence along Woodward Avenue. Today, the one-time street racing venue is mostly quiet and high-speed cruising is strictly prohibited. ©1997 Tom Shaw/Musclecar Review Magazine

tain that you drove the "fastest set of wheels in town," it was unwise to put up title to your little deuce coupe when you were racing an unknown challenger. With all the races being run for real scratch, there were more than a few clever hustlers haunting the streets. These crafty guys drove cars known as "sleepers," vehicles that looked like a decrepit dog on the outside yet had all the workings of a thoroughbred on the inside. "I bit off a little more than I could chew back in 1958," groaned Seattlite Parker Jones, relating the story of how his 1957 Chevy once got stomped by a 1932 highboy with primer. "These days, as a commercial insurance underwriter, I'm a helluva lot more aware of risks than I was during the fifties. I never would have agreed to race that guy who rolled into the Aurora A & W with that ragged old heap had I known what was hiding underneath his hood! It's a good thing we were only racing for a twenty!"

In the same vein of deception, there were a few "posers" who just liked the *idea* of street racing and the benefits it promised. Dean Batchelor in his book *The American Hot Rod* related the ploy such posers would use to fool onlookers into thinking they owned a souped-up car. First, they wheeled into the drive-in lot and parked in a prominent spot. Then, they pulled the hand brake, depressed the clutch, and threw the transmission into second gear. Next, they turned the ignition key off as they removed their foot from the clutch pedal! With the ignition disconnected, the clutch dragged up against the flywheel, causing the motor to stop turning. Since the racers in the know were well aware that mills with high compression (and extra power) had light flywheels, those that stopped right after the ignition cut off were most likely modified. Peers who watched from the sidelines became duped into believing that the car was a hot one and that the driver was waiting for the next race (it never came).

By the 1960s, differentiating between the real racers and posers became even more complicated. To the delight of enthusiasts, the stock production vehicles made in America began to change. What had begun 10 years earlier as a skirmish among U.S. automakers to build mod-

The running joke among cruisers has always been that if you want to find a cop, just head to the local doughnut shop. During the sixties, the doughnut shop offered hot rodders, hippies, customizers, lowriders, bikers, and even the law a no-man's land that was free from hassle. At the same service counter, a diverse range of individuals could enjoy a cup of coffee and a glazed doughnut. Even so, this wasn't the place to burn rubber. *Kent Bash*

mag wheels, whiskey, speed equipment, switchblades, and seat covers. On rare occasions, girls were the racer's bounty! Most racing was for cold hard cash where winner took all (unless you were driving against a townie, it was best to have a neutral third party hold the green). Sometimes, street rodders raced head-to-head for pink slips, the postwar equivalent of today's car titles. Whoever won took ownership of the other rodder's car—and its speed secrets.

This combo of cars and high-stakes betting was a risky proposition at best. Unless you knew for cer-

ern, eight-cylinder, overhead-valve motors ended in an industrywide battle for more horsepower and cubic inches! For consumers, the war of automotive supremacy was a dream come true: Many of the performance specs written by hot rod buffs in the back alleys and garages became a part of Detroit's mass-production repertoire. At last, the establishment had acknowledged that cars weren't just a mere practical means of transportation. As legions of street racers and cruisers had tried to demonstrate for so many years, the car was a great gadget for recreation and sport!

In the new decade Pontiac chief engineer John DeLorean introduced a new type of hybrid automobile that combined cool looks and power in one hot package. Taking inspiration from the cadre of illegal street racers shredding the asphalt on Detroit's Woodward Boulevard, DeLorean and his engineers yanked the four-banger from the Tempest model and dropped in a 389-cubic-inch V-8 as replacement. At the same time, they stiffened the suspension and added heavy-duty brakes. Intrigued by the flash of the Italian sports car scene, he "borrowed" Ferrari's exotic-sounding "Gran Turismo Omologato" name from its racing 250 and lifted the lead letters to make his own memorable model name in 1964: GTO. With a mystique all their own, 60,000 Pontiac GTOs thundered out of the factory and onto America's streets. The youth market responded favorably to the $2,500 price tag. Within two years, DeLorean's performance vision became Detroit's best-selling muscle car.

By the time Ronny and the Daytonas debuted their musical homage *Little GTO* in 1964, all of Detroit's automobile manufacturers were developing their own muscles. Shortly thereafter, baby boomers who could afford the monthly payments were snapping up fast-sounding names such as Mustang, Barracuda, Charger, Road Runner, and Camaro. At last, carmakers were assembling fully warranted versions of the passenger coupe, sports car, and hot rod all rolled into one fast, unified package. The new configuration looked to be so popular that even the *Little Old Lady from Pasadena* drove a brand new shiny red Super-Stock Dodge.

Power cruisers knew the Beach Boys' lyrics by heart: "She drives real fast and she drives real hard, she's a terror out on Colorado Boulevard. . . ." With dual exhausts, powerful engines, and four-on-the-floor transmissions, muscle cars were definitely a hit.

Suddenly, production-line racers outnumbered homemade hot rods at the illegal racing venues. Now, it was hot rods against muscle cars, old values versus new. The philosophical concerns about cars became a dividing line between participants: Was a homemade street rod the only way to go? Was a financed purchase from the local car dealer another way to get a racer? The questions were moot. By the mid-sixties, most of the hot rodding purists had gone into hibernation. The war in Vietnam played a big part, since a lot of shade-tree mechanics and hot rodders shipped out overseas. Reduced to dreaming of rods and customs that might have been, departing servicemen passed the ignition keys on to their little brothers. Within the first week, wrecks claimed many cars. More wore out from too much use and a lack of maintenance. Parents sold off the rest after Johnny failed to come marching home again.

Of the hot rods that managed to survive the turmoil of the times, many became so radically modified for dragstrip racing and speed trials that legal cruising on the public streets was out of the question. A victim of continual upgrading, some of the best sported chrome and other expensive goodies and were dressed to the nines. Now, they were far too valuable for casual, everyday cruising in the streets. With their rarity increasing daily, many classic rods headed for static exhibition on the

continued on page 97

NEXT: A scurrilous pack of muscle machines taking over the streets was at one time the bane of Detroit's cops and citizens. Out along the neon-bathed miles of Woodward Avenue, dozens of racing match-ups could be made within the span of an hour. All one had to do was cruise the strip and look for them. When one encountered an able-looking competitor in traffic, the two cars lined up and went for it until traffic congestion or stop lights caused one or the other to break off. In the realm of street racing, there was nothing like it. ©*1997 Tom Shaw*/Musclecar Review Magazine

Continued from page 93

Detroit, Michigan, became the capital of street racing during the sixties and gained national notoriety for Woodward Avenue. On any given night, muscle cars like this 1969 Dodge Charger and 1970 Chevelle Super Sport 396 could be found doing battle on the streets of the "Motor City." *Kent Bash*

custom show car circuit—never to be taken out into traffic again! For the time being, the hot rod traditions begun so many years ago were on hold.

In the meantime, muscle cars took over the spotlight and by their mere presence, caused more than a few streets to achieve the status of street racing legend. In Motor City Detroit, Michigan, Woodward Avenue ascended to the throne as the undisputed king of America's illegal dragstrips. In September 1967, writer Brock Yates acknowledged this royal lineage of drag racing in *Car and Driver* magazine, dubbing Woodward Avenue the "street racing capital of the world." Almost 30 years later, *Musclecar Review* magazine editor Tom Shaw reiterated the bold claim in his article, "The Kings of Woodward Avenue." His words tell it all: "There were hot streets in most every town in America, but there was only one Woodward, and the Woodward experience was unlike any other. It was frats versus greasers, north versus south, east versus west, club versus club, GM versus Mopar versus Ford, man versus man, man versus woman, and man versus himself. I'll tell you what Woodward was—it was a real-life movie we all starred in. Too bad nobody made it, because it would have blown *American Graffiti* in the weeds."

As exciting as the ambiance was for car nuts, the authorities didn't much appreciate the no-holds-barred carnival atmosphere of illegal, unchecked street racing on Woodward! By the mid-seventies, serious plans to curtail the fun were being implemented. The first blow was an ordinance that banned customers from car-hopping, or leaving their cars on foot while parked at an eatery. To guarantee against the building of new hangouts, the city fathers outlawed drive-ins! About that time, the police also cracked down on racing: Minor traffic violations like a "display of speed" or rolling a yellow resulted in hefty fines. After realizing that illegal racing provided

big revenues, cops began handing out traffic tickets like advertising circulars! Street racers headed for the pits—hit in the wallet where it hurt the most. Competition in public was no longer economically viable and the circuit returned to commuters.

After the mass exodus, the fantasy of driving a muscle car began to shed a lot of its star dust. In 1969, all the illusions shattered when insurance agents nationwide read a report published in *The Reflector* (an insurance industry magazine). "What's Behind the Surcharge" showed that so-called muscle cars would comprise just 6 percent of the total car market for the coming year. Despite this, researchers pointed to the fact that vehicles with engines over 300 horsepower would be responsible for 56 percent more monetary losses than ordinary passenger vehicles! Categorizing America's muscle machines as "overpowered," both the Nationwide and State Farm insurance companies planned to institute a 25 to 50 percent surcharge on the insurance purchased to cover these so-called death machines. Now, performance cars had a price on their heads.

Two years later, the chase thriller *Vanishing Point* debuted at America's drive-in theaters and paid a farewell tribute to the era of powerful cars. In the film, actor Barry Newman starred as Kowalski, one of the "last American heroes," a car delivery driver intent on winning a bet regarding his arrival time after taking a supercharged white Dodge Challenger cross country. In spite of the smashed roadblocks and the trail of mayhem left in his wake, the white knight's final "run" became an ironic allegory for the demise of the muscle car.

Even fearless Kowalski couldn't outrun hungry insurance companies and greedy oil men. In October 1973, an embargo on all petroleum shipments made to the United States began. The next day, the Organization of Petroleum Exporting Countries (OPEC) decided to raise crude prices by a shocking 70 percent! Overnight, gas prices doubled to more than $1 per gallon. Long lines, gas rationing plans, and overheated tempers followed. Forced out by economics and killjoy authorities, American street racing, the muscle car, and wasting gas ground to a halt.

Strutting Their Stuff on the Street

America's Automotive Exhibitionists

"Creating an identity by way of one's automobile is a personal thing. For some, it's the fancy aftermarket goodies, expensive custom bodywork, and the act of displaying that prosperity out on the streets. For others, it's the fun that can be had by doing all of the work yourself and learning a variety of crafts along the way, while enjoying the camaraderie of friends. This scenario of friends helping out friends is what I remember best from hot rodding's heyday in the fifties. It's still important today.

I know about cutting corners when building cars because I saw my brother Mel paint his first hot rod all by himself. It was a nice, Model A roadster with no fenders and a '48 flathead engine. As a teenager slaving away to earn some money at the local Burger Bar flipping burgers, he really couldn't save up the extra cash he needed for a good paint job. So, he decided to take the simplest route and do a homemade job right in our driveway.

After deciding on a color, he picked up the paint he needed from a local paint supply shop, then stopped at the hardware store to pick up a brush. He sanded and prepped the car as best he could and carefully applied a few coats of paint to build up the thickness. When all of the layers finally dried, he finish-sanded the body to smooth out the brush marks and then rubbed it out with plenty of elbow grease until it shone. The crazy thing was, I couldn't really tell any difference between his work and a high-dollar, spray-painted job! From my limited perspective of youth and inexperience, it was one of the keenest paint jobs that I had ever seen. To me, it sparkled with professionalism.

But that wasn't the only thing he did to make his rod unique. The homemade scheme of decorating and customizing continued on the inside of Mel's car. For quick and simple seat covers, he bought a really cool Indian blanket and threw it over the worn seat covers and rips. It might sound like a tacky method when compared to the elaborate upholstery work that's done today—but back then, a lot of cruisers used blankets to make their cars more comfortable. In a pinch, even green Army blankets did the trick.

It all goes back to the same thing: During the early days of hot rods and custom cars, the simple fact that a guy owned a car and had the freedom to go wherever he wanted to go was a lot more important than having the ultimate engine, flame job, interior, or wheels. Besides, once you had the money and could go out and buy all those goodies, a little bit of the magic was lost. Unjaded, it was the dreaming of things to come that mattered the most."
—*Kent Bash*

A set of personalized cruising compartments: a 1932 Ford Roadster and 1949 Oldsmobile Rocket 88, parked at Barkie's famous roadside hot dog stand on West Washington Boulevard in Los Angeles. In 1951, one year before Oldsmobile introduced this brand new, streamlined, Hydra-Matic, eight-cylinder dream machine, Jackie Brenston with His Delta Cats came out with the song Rocket 88, a rock and roll tune that could well have served as an anthem for the custom creed. As a pickup machine, how could an ordinary hot rod compare when one considered the plush seats, comfortable ride, and styling of the first "rocket" engine Olds? The song's hook promised cruisers the world: "You women have heard of jalopies, you've heard the noise they make, well let me introduce you to my rocket 88, . . . baby we'll ride in style." In the world of cars, cruising, and picking up chicks, the custom was king. *Kent Bash*

UP from the rubble of the gasoline-gobbling muscle car era rose a movement to resurrect the dormant hot rod arts of the forties and fifties. As America witnessed the effects of the sexual revolution and the disco descent of rock and roll, the mavens of customized car shows and other exhibitions broke with convention and started taking their show-quality roadsters, coupes, and convertibles out on the asphalt in ever-increasing numbers. Cruising was back!

Driving and displaying their precious cars in public so that other people could see them, loyalists in California took it upon themselves to spread the gospel of cruising up and down the West Coast and then across the continent—re-energizing all of the backsliders across America. Organized motoring clubs like the San Francisco Bay Area Roadsters and Los Angeles Roadsters were at the forefront of the revved-up revival. Taking to the streets whenever and wherever they could, these reborn cruisers sought to disprove the exaggerated reports of the hot rodder's demise!

As American rodders rediscovered their roots, a wave of publicity primed the car crowd's interest. Major motoring magazines like *Hot Rod*, *Car Craft*, and *Street Rodder* began touting the rod and custom formats with renewed vigor. To widen interest, the pundits considered "new" ideas: Could mass-produced, affordable cars (made during the fifties) be considered a starting point for traditional custom projects? The hobby was ripe for expansion, and

With radically restyled taillights, this late-forties Chevrolet custom exemplifies some of the custom work executed during the fifties. Back then, many car builders did extensive rework in areas like the headlights and taillights but left the rest of the car pretty much untouched. *Kent Bash/car courtesy George Killger*

cruising activities began to blossom. "Rod runs" were the newest rage and every type of car under the sun was welcome. "It used to be that only certain cars were thought of as customs but now, many more may be thought about when building a custom car," explained Max Klaus, a cruiser from Germany who makes regular trips to the states to drive the length of Route 66. "In the United States, the group that is called Kustom Kemps of America limits the custom cars to body styles that were stamped out between 1936 and 1964. 'Kemp' was used to refer to cars back during the fifties, it was a beatnik slang word."

In 1970, the good folks at *Rod & Custom* magazine (one of the more vocal periodicals that supported the pastime) sponsored what became the first important national gathering for the hobby. A farmer's field in Peoria, Illinois, was the point of convergence for the highly publicized motoring meet. From all corners of the map, more than 600 hairy hot rods and curvy customs cruised out to America's Heartland. Those who were lucky enough to attend this Woodstock of wheels reveled in the real, motorized sounds of "heavy metal" and witnessed for themselves that the interest in building personalized cars was still goin' strong. Better still, it appeared that the denizens of America's drive-in culture were returning once more to the main core of the cruising philosophy: Driving the strip in an attention-getting vehicle was a helluva lot of fun!

As hot rods made their reappearance, the attitudes toward cruising and cars were changing dramatically. Once a pastime, drag racing had evolved into a big-money, professional sport with corporate sponsors and wide appeal. With the counterculture image somewhat watered down, many cruisers became jaded to the idea of street racing. More important, all of the classic cars that lived through the Vietnam years were worth a lot more money than they used to be. Risking a car crash to prove yourself to another reckless rodder was stupid! Older, wiser, and married with children, former risk-takers now had homes, full-time jobs, and mortgage payments. Sadly, a few had to sell their cars. "With a baby on the way, I didn't have a choice. I had to sell my first roadster,"

Junkyards, salvage sellers, and dumps were the point of birth for many of the classic road machines of the forties, fifties, and sixties. True, new car dealers had some of the best cars in town, but cars built with sweat and imagination were always cooler. *Mike Witzel*

The Pele was a car developed by the Kaiser Aluminum Company during the fifties as an answer to the durable body shell. Body panels were made of stamped aluminum sheet with enameled finish, with side trim of brushed and gold-colored anodized aluminum. Bumpers, roof rails, and the top roof panel were all of aluminum. Wraparound glass was used extensively. During the postwar years, automakers began dreaming up—and building—features that were previously only in the minds of customizers. *Courtesy of the Automotive Hall of Fame*

In the fifties, cruising over the horizon were the automotive attributes Speed and Beauty, a set of parents that would bear a car-crazed America a wondrous new offspring. From the dream factories of Detroit, fabulous concept cars came off the drawing boards and captured the public's attention at car shows and other demonstrations. Some, like General Motor's famed Golden Rocket, were far too extravagant and customized for their time, and as a result, the models never made it into full-scale production. *Courtesy of the Automotive Hall of Fame*

moaned Charles Vandreason, attendee of a recent cruise event near Rancho Cucamonga, California. "If I could have had it my way, I would have kept that car and figured some other way of gettin' up some money. I love my kids, but I will never forget that old Lincoln heap or find another one quite like it!"

With wild-eyed competition no longer the main interest of garage-bound enthusiasts, the hopped-up, slicked out street rod became just another expensive plaything in the adult toy box. Not even the hot rod's racing roots could negate its taming. This was a considerable change from decades past, when the sole intent of America's

backyard car builders was to emphasize *speed* over *looks*. During the hurly-burly days of time trials, competitors knew the drill: You had to eliminate parts if they didn't make a car go any faster! To minimize weight, racers removed nonessentials like the trim, mirrors, running boards, door handles, fenders, and the hood ornaments. To decrease wind resistance, roofs were "chopped" and bodies "channeled" (to allow the body to sit lower on the frame). Later, when the racing rabble roared into the streets, car builders continued the speed-inspired styling techniques largely out of habit. By that time, America's hot rods were beginning to look a lot less like the racing machines that they

Imagine the Chevrolet Corvette completely customized with a mild Jetsons influence and a touch of the hot rodder's art thrown in for good measure. It happened in this fifties concept version of a Corvette, a rather outlandish idea that, fortunately, never saw life on the streets. *Courtesy of the Automotive Hall of Fame*

off the *ride* and turn the *cars* into the competition. It was the visual aspect of cruising that was important, so there wasn't any need to prove mechanical ability. Instead of dancing around the streets to find opponents, those in the custom club drove leisurely down the Main, moving slow enough to see onlooker reactions. For them, speeding tickets were rare. Citations for "impeding traffic" were more likely.

Nevertheless, the customizers still had to prove their status within their own group. Playing to a street-side audience was an important ritual for owners of customized machines, just as participating in a street race was for those infatuated with hot rods. For automotive exhibitionists, the quest for perfection showed a single-minded, manic fervor. Who cared about the horsepower of the engine, the displacement of the piston, or number of carburetors? It was the outside window dressings that transformed an ordinary, clunky coupe into a cool car, and as a result, it was these image-shaping elements that held priority over engine and mechanical work. To elicit a favorable response from the peanut gallery along the Main Street sidewalk, a car's upholstery, exterior paint, and wheel coverings demanded top billing.

After World War II, it was the same self-conscious attitude that led custom car artists to follow America's hot rodders to the junkyards. There, they found that most of the second-hand motoring stock was all but gone. The throng of hop-up hounds bent on building racing roadsters and fast street rods had already snatched up most of the smaller, lightweight cars. Even so, the shortage wasn't a big problem, since the end-product made by the custom crowd relied on the cars that were available—namely, the enclosed vehicles manufactured during the late thirties and early forties that were ill-suited for drag racing. If one

originally started out as. More and more, these insolent chariots resembled the automobiles known as "customs."

The stylistic evolution was important to the cruising hobby, as the Main Street strip was obviously more suited toward the display of cars than it was racing. For the pastime of cruising to gain a wide audience from all types of car owners, it had to lose some of the negative associations linked with hard-core hot rodding. Custom cars and their emphasis on style would go a long way in convincing skeptics that cruising wasn't a disruptive activity. At the same time, a heated clan rivalry between America's customizers and hot rodders had been simmering since the glory days of water bags and hood ornaments. It was an age-old conflict: The hot rodder liked to go fast and turn every run into some sort of competition, while customizers liked to take it slow and easy. Hot rod fans were big on motors, mechanics, and parts that equaled speed. In contrast, the customizer's "thing" was to show

This highly reflective and customized Ford is chopped, channeled, and sectioned with a pancaked hood. The headlights are frenched and the body is so low that the height of the entire car only comes up to your waist. It was this type of car that attracted the attention of the cruisers and crowds. *Kent Bash*

Decked out with massive flame work, minimurals, and running a Chevy drivetrain, this 1949 Mercury is a great example of a mild custom. In the spirit of the great American customizers, who often come up with cool-sounding names like *Chezoom*, *Cadzilla*, and so on, this custom creation is called *Mercula*. *Kent Bash/car courtesy Dave King*

The massive whales made between the years 1949 and 1951 under the Mercury marque became prized commodities for the cruiser and customizer (it was somewhat ironic that these slow cruisin' favorites took the same name of the mythical god of speed). These babies were real driving cars—big, brash, bulbous—with curves in all the right places! ©1997 Andy Southard

desired to lighten up these heavy cars, there wasn't a good way to cut away parts without making the body look ridiculous. With the integrated bodies these cars wore, the rakish stance of the stripped hot rod just didn't work.

None of this mattered to the customizer. Cruisers fell in love with the bigger, more stylish cars for the comfortable ride and massive visual presence they afforded. As a creative canvas, a few models became hands-down favorites, most notably the 1936 Ford. With a curvaceous design that diverged from models of previous years, it encouraged the customizer's creativity and just begged for extra body modifications and restyling. A few years down the road, the massive whales made by Mercury between the years 1940 and 1951 became prized commodities, too (it was ironic that these slow cruisin' favorites had the same name as the mythical god of speed). These were real driving cars—big, brash, bulbous—with curves in all the right places. Perfectly suited for recreational cruising, customizers adored them.

Automotive author/photographer and long-time Mercury lover Andy Southard remains one of the brand's loyal followers. "I had a 1940 Mercury coupe 'stocker' when I was going to high school," he reminisced. "This was in 1949. I sold it and then had another car, a '49 Ford. Then, I always used to think, Why did I sell my Mercury? I loved it so much that I decided someday I would get another one. Well time went on—40-some years— and I was able to buy this '40 Mercury that I have now! I had a friend of mine who does bodywork, Tom Cutino, do all the customizing. He chopped the top, molded the fenders, and put in electric openers in the doors and the trunk. He installed a 350 Chevrolet engine with an automatic transmission, and, as the style of the period was in 1949, teardrop fender skirts. Underneath, it's all brand new, but by outward appearances, it's the same customized Mercury that you would have seen on the strip during the forties."

With life-long devotees like this, the Mercury brand attained a marked measure of popularity

Architect Mies Van Der Rohe once stated that "God is in the details." While he didn't have automobiles in mind when he uttered these words, it certainly would be true for many custom cars and hot rods. For the automotive aficionado, the simple routing of spark plug wires could turn into an expression of art, and the finishing touches in an engine compartment can be as important as the body. ©1997 Robert Genat

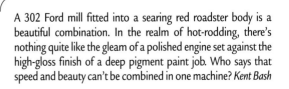
An original, far out paint job is one feature of an automobile that's guaranteed to get attention out in the streets. Hot rodders, lowriders, and customizers all regard the paint job as an important part of the cruising scene. *Mike Witzel*

A 302 Ford mill fitted into a searing red roadster body is a beautiful combination. In the realm of hot-rodding, there's nothing quite like the gleam of a polished engine set against the high-gloss finish of a deep pigment paint job. Who says that speed and beauty can't be combined in one machine? *Kent Bash*

A lowered "resto rod" running Centerline wheels, this 1937 Chevy Coupe is a popular hot rod look. Throughout the years, manufacturers have turned out body styles that were nice enough to leave stock. For those who desire an extra touch, a modern drivetrain and flashy paint job are all that is needed to customize cars like this. *Kent Bash*

among cruisers. Eventually, it was the brand that came to mind whenever someone uttered "customs and cruising" in the same breath. It became such a notorious part of drive-in lore that in 1976, the Steve Miller Band acknowledged the following with a rendition of K. C. Johnson's *Mercury Blues*. One particular verse of the old standard confirmed the babe-pulling power of a tricked-out Merc: "You know that gal I love, I stole her from a friend, fool got lucky stole her back again. Because she knowed he had a Mercury, cruise up and down this road, up and down this road. Well, she knowed he had a Mercury, and she cruise up and down this road." Whether stock or custom, the Mercury had the ephemeral quality that attracted members of the opposite sex.

Despite the numerous songs being written about their romantic qualities, the oversized highway cars like the Fords and Mercurys didn't gain a reputation as love machines. In fact, custom cars became known as "lead sleds!" Despite the somewhat negative connotation, it was a good description, since many cruisers will tell you that the nickname originated from the early coach workers and auto body repairmen who first used molten lead to fill body imperfections and smooth out welds, today, bodywork is done with the plastic filler Bondo. As it happened, custom fans borrowed the regimen during the forties and fifties and used it to shape body contours, patch small dents, and to level connecting seams. Adding weight became a known side-effect of building a custom.

Not everyone saw this added weight as an asset. Like a straight man who waits for his punch line, customizers and their overloaded rides frequently became the butt of jokes whenever jealous hot rodders were around. Those who preferred to "go over show" used the term to denigrate the custom owner every chance they could. "One time on Sepulveda Boulevard, a hot rodder pointed in the direction of my hood and inquired if I had my mama's sewing machine mounted in there," recalled Tim Wisemann, a present-day custom car fan and occasional California cruiser. "I felt like socking him in the mouth, but I took it for what it was, just another jealous comment from a guy that wouldn't know what style was if it hit him right between the eyes." Most of the sarcastic jibes fell on deaf ears, because ardent custom fans didn't give them much credence. They were too busy building a motorized Disneyland for themselves that provided the maximum cruising experience.

The process of turning an ordinary car into a custom was rarely as easy as slapping on new accessories. More often than not, it took a lot of hard work and patience to transform an automobile into the ultimate cruising coach. The changes ran the gamut from minor cosmetic fixes to major bodywork. Car guys (and some gals) referred to simple refinements as mild and extensive reworks as wild. In the mild category, the customizer handy with tools often modified the suspension or cut the coils to make the car hug the asphalt. (At first, customizers dropped the rear and the front remained high.) With a nip here and a tuck there, the body got a face-lift with subtle changes. Maybe it was the sloping line of a fender that changed or, possibly, the crease of the hood. Perhaps it was the way the door panel connected with the rest of the body. And why not hide the gas filler neck in the trunk or employ a few other unexpected tricks? Nothing was off limits! The extent and complexity of rework depended on the fantasy that came alive in the mind's eye of the customizer and his or her ability.

When deciding what changes to make, it didn't take a rocket scientist to figure out what looked cool and what didn't. If one chopped the car's roof or channeled the body, the ride fell on the wild side of custom. Occasionally, cruisers crafted new body segments for this type of vehicle from scratch and replaced the original fenders, hoods,

or rear quarter panels. Swapping nice parts from completely different brands was an acceptable practice, too. Cruisers exchanged bumpers and front grilles like library books. Occasionally, minor surgery allowed the wheel cutouts to conform more perfectly with the circumference of the tires. Custom guys referred to these modified wheel openings as "radiused."

When a custom owner wanted to go beyond the norm and make a bold statement to boot, the automobile was "sectioned." This severe technique was no job for an amateur bodyman, however,

since it called for the careful removal of all excess material around the horizontal axis of the vehicle! If done right, the creation was reborn from the custom shop as a flatter, more sinister version of the original car. "Say you take three inches out of the car, you don't actually do it on all the panels in the same spot," explained Scott Guildner, a prominent Van Nuys, California, customizer. "You might cut the door in the middle and the quarter panel down at the bottom—whatever area is flattest and most vertical. If you do it on an angled area you

This custom Mercury is not really what it seems to be. At a glance, it appears that the curve above the lake pipe is outfitted with an accent of chrome. Closer examination reveals the customizer's secret: The polished metal is actually a skillful application of paint! With custom cars, nothing should be taken for granted. *Kent Bash*

Tom Otis, or "Quickdraw" as his business card describes him, spends his days crafting hot rods, spraying paint, and applying pinstriping. Here, the maestro is seen applying the finishing touches to his 1932 Ford Roadster. Whether it's done to a custom car or a hot rod, pinstriping provides the finishing touch needed to make an automobile stand out. *Kent Bash*

Anyone who has taken a shop class in high school knows that the central creed of surface finishing is sanding, sanding, and finally—more sanding. Here Jeff Tann's 1936 Ford is getting the full treatment. *Kent Bash*

may have problems. When you bring the part down, it might not match up. Either way, it's a lot of work!"

Naturally, customizers came up with their own terms for some of these body modifications, adding their own page of slang to the American cruising dictionary. Many of these descriptions are still in use today, and new ones are still being invented. If a car was "nosed," it didn't have hood emblems or ornaments to detract from the streamlined look. At the tail end, a "decked" trunk showed no sign of placards or mounting holes. Enthusiasts filled, sanded, and painted over them. On each body side, "shaved" door panels had nothing to do with the grooming habits of the cruiser. Among customizers, it referred to the fact that no door handles showed. Like all of the other techniques used to make the body as smooth as possible, it added an extra touch that set a car apart from the crowd. To access the car, one reached inside the window or used remote-controlled, electrical solenoids to activate the latches. Custom cruisers figured out other ways to get noticed. Among the most widely used effects were frenched headlight and taillight housings. This sexy-sounding technique allowed for the installation of the lamp lenses from the rear, in an alluring, recessed manner, without trim.

Wheels were a big deal, too. Where the hot rod might be outfitted with "big 'n littles" (small wheels mounted in the front and large ones in the back) both wild and mild customs could have no less than whitewall tires all the way around. Often, fender skirts covered up most of the rear wheels, adding to the look of the laminar flow. Despite the hidden rear wheels, most hard-core custom owners cherished certain wheel covers. Excited by the eye-catching layout of light-reflecting ridges, cruisers went ga-ga over the full-sized "flippers" found on the 1956 Olds Fiesta and late-model Dodge Lancers. During the crazy years of the fifties, some guys pushed the limits of creativity when they modified their wheel pans with faucet handles and drawer pulls! Regardless of the style, size, finish, or

This 1958 Volkswagen was co-author Kent Bash's fourth work in the mobile medium, a job that took him some 5,000 hours to paint by hand. The first year that Bash put his "art you can drive" on the street, he received 80 traffic tickets (only one conviction) for a wide variety of nonmoving violations. Sometimes, he even got tickets on the way to paying other tickets. A total of six Volkswagen Beetles were used for the mobile art series, most of which have been wrecked. Today, they are a prime example that the car was and still is a perfect canvas to express one's imagination and personality—even if it does mean getting cited for the privilege. *Kent Bash*

decoration, the lug nut covers once taken for granted became totems for creative cruise culture.

Within the tribe, full wheel covers became a requirement, led by the sombrero-style hubcaps borrowed from Cadillacs of 1949 to 1953 vintage. This bent for Caddy rim covers became the bane of ordinary car owners who happened to own a car manufactured within this span of years. Houston, Texas, bodyshop man Slim Waters was a witness to the theft, recalling problems his own father had with wheel covers. "Yessir, my pa had himself a big old Cadillac and along with it a world of hurt. He got his hubcaps stolen twice! The first time, he was travelin' when they was lifted near Eldorado, Kansas, while he was stayin' at a cheap motel. The other time, he caught the guy in the act when some kid tried to pop 'em off right in our own driveway! You never seen a body move so fast tryin' to get outta' the way of two

The Toed Inn was one of those quirky roadside restaurants of the 1920s. In those exciting days, mom-and-pop eateries with unique personalities filled up the roadsides and provided cruising havens for hot rods and custom cars. Long before fast food franchising took over the process of roadside dining, sandwich stands like this programmatic marvel were packed with cars—including some like these gleaming 1940 and 1941 Willys models. *Kent Bash*

barrels full of buckshot!" During the days of the juvenile delinquent, the "midnight auto supply" provided many cruisers with free parts.

When they weren't busy combing the streets and salvage yards for the right hubcaps, America's hot rod Picassos and custom-car Modiglianis used their extra time to develop a signature style of car painting. Unlike commercial auto manufacturers, customizers went out of their way to avoid using ordinary patterns and colors. From the suede-black primer of an unfinished hot rod to the purple radiance of a multilayer custom, the devotion to exterior shading was strong. "You can't rush it," warned

West Coast custom enthusiast Randy "Snake" Chadd. "Preparation is eight months and painting is three hours. It's just a matter of how good you want it to look. A friend wanted me to paint his car and said he didn't want it to be a real 'good' paint job, and I told him I don't know how to do any other kind! You just don't paint a car, you paint it right—that's my philosophy." It's a sentiment shared by many, as some painters believe they can transfer the personality of a car owner onto body metal with a careful application of color and pattern.

During the fifties, bodyman Joe Bailon revitalized the field of automotive painting after he devised a new paint color called Candy Apple Red. While experimenting in his Oakland, California, shop, he discovered a unique car finish by adding just a few drops of red liquid toner to clear lacquer. Bailon sprayed layer upon layer of the hybrid mixture over a gold base and discovered he had a stunning new finish. It was pure magic, since the paint looked wet even after the tinted lacquer dried! It didn't take long for the customizers to get the hots for this translucent lip-gloss look, and soon they were spraying it onto cars like nobody's business. The pearlescent variation of the candy color became a favorite. Originally, car painters blended finely ground fish scales with different shades of lacquer to create the pearlized effect (later, they substituted ingredients that were easier to obtain). After numerous applica-

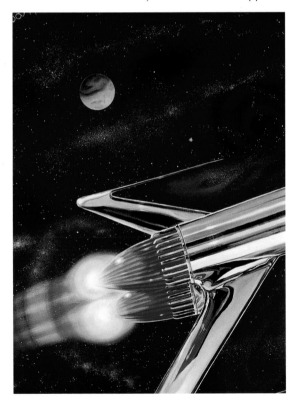

The tail fin is one of the most visible symbols of the design changes that occurred in cars during the fifties. Influenced by aircraft like the P-38, Detroit designers (such as Harley Earl) added aerodynamic visuals to their car bodies as a way of embracing the future and the promise that it might hold. Today, tail fins are potent reminders of yesterday's bold styling and flamboyant designs. *Kent Bash*

tions of paint dried, the dichroic fragments of overlapping material reflected light in the very same manner as mother-of-pearl. More daring car artists took the idea to the edge of tackiness when they used tiny shards of aluminum foil for the reflecting medium. All the rage during the sixties, customizers of present day use the metal-flake finish sparingly.

By the beginning of the 1960s, America's customizers had a tasty sampler of candies from which to choose. Improved acrylic resins gave commercial car manufacturers new choices as well. Now, there was no longer an excuse to paint a vehicle in the somber tones of yesteryear. Suddenly, a big can of Kool-Aid color, a Bink's spray gun, and an air compressor endowed the car artist with limitless creative options. As custom vehicles (and later some hot rods) began to incorporate the new look, painting an automobile changed from a boring, production line step to a bona fide expression of art.

Still, it wasn't as easy as just dipping a paintbrush into a bucket of paint (although many tried just that). To achieve the perfect, flawless finish, the craft of painting required a lot of patient practice. Even the experienced custom automobile builders

The Rocket 88 Oldsmobile—the predecessor to the radical fin jobs to be introduced in the early fifties—was a car that exhibited the sort of "jukebox" ornamentation that typified many of motoring machines of the late forties and the early fifties. In the early days, hot rodders disdained this ornamentation and stripped away all chrome and molding in the interest of speed. *Kent Bash*

While Chevrolets were available in some great color schemes during the 1950s, no commercial units were sold in this custom hot pink configuration. These days, cars frequently cross over into the category of custom—even if they don't have extensive bodywork or structural changes. All it takes to make the trip to the wild side is some crazy colors and a spray gun. ©1997 Robert Genat

The 1957 Chevrolet Bel Air remains one of the all-time favorites among cruisers who prefer their cars stock. No cruise night or trip down Main Street would be complete without seeing one of these finned beauties in action. Mike Witzel

Randy "Snake" Chadd chopping the top on a 1942 Ford Coupe. Chadd earned the unusual nickname because all of his vehicles run as low "as a snake on the grass." For a low-cost, effective security system, he often lets a few Burmese pythons loose in his car! It's a great way to keep hands off when his ride is parked at the neighborhood cruise night! Kent Bash

Contrary to macho beliefs, cruising is a pastime that's enjoyed by both sexes. Here, Gilda Hendrickson shows off her 1939 pickup, a slightly lowered ride that features a Chevy drivetrain and a custom paint treatment. *Kent Bash*

paid for their mistakes in lost time and money. Unlike the home-built hot rods assembled by trial and error, customizers sometimes used brand new automobiles as the starting point. With a major investment like that, it was best to do it right the first time.

As a result, many professional custom car shops opened their doors to offer a wide range of creative services to cruisers. One of the most successful was begun by brothers George and Sam Barris in Los Angeles, California. By the mid-fifties, the Barris Kustom Shop gained recognition with customized beauties like the *Hirohata Mercury* and *Golden Sahara*—setting new standards for the custom car builder to live up to. But that wasn't all: Barris expanded the creative parameters of the craft even further when he unveiled way-out concept cars the likes of *Miss Elegance*, *Ala Kart*, and *Fabula*. Under his direction, one-of-a-kind wheels squealed onto the silver screen and into that little box called television. Who can forget *Batman*, *The Munsters*, and *My Mother the Car*? All these shows

and many movies featured Barris creations. As a custom master, he proved the hypothesis that the car was sculpture, inspiring a new generation to create its own interpretation of mobile art.

Kenneth Howard, or "Von Dutch," as his admirers called him, was another one of customizing's great innovators. During the fifties, he became the undisputed guru of pinstriping and defined the art of decorating the car. It all started after he borrowed his father's sign-painting materials and followed his own muse on an automotive canvas. With all the skill of a great master, he proceeded to apply complex pinstriping as an addition to paint and body styling—embellishing curves and corners with abstract crests. While only he understood what the ligatures meant, the customizer's eyeballs popped out (like a crazy cartoon character) when they saw them. It was the correct response, considering that it was Von Dutch himself who created the famous "flying eyeball" that the cruisin' crowd adopted as the hobby's unofficial icon (today, it's still seen on hot rods and customs, and one can even buy shift knobs made in the form of the disembodied peeper).

Another one of Von Dutch's specialties was decorative markings known as "scallops." Applied over the base color of a car, the scallop treatment looked

This 1955 Chevrolet sports a hot 1991 Corvette 350 engine with aluminum heads. While not a vintage mill, this powerplant gives the custom the get-up-and-go that's required to hold its own among the power-hungry roadsters cruising the strip. A polished, tuned-port electronic fuel injection system is part of the configuration, as are stainless steel Corvette headers. *Mike Witzel/car courtesy Clare Patterson, Jr.*

like a planned arrangement of schizophrenic pinstriping. At their most extreme, these reverse-tip, airbrushed daggers (with carefully painted borders) ran along the entire length of a custom automobile, covering most of the hood area, body side panels, and the trunk lid. Since the heavily bordered arrangements distracted the viewer's eyeballs from slight body imperfections, the scallop technique became the saving grace for inexperienced body workers. Most of the time, scallops were an optical trick more than they were a painterly effect.

To make a car look really hot—literally—painted flames were a great substitute for scallops and flying eyeballs. A sheet of flames painted on the hood (and sometimes the body side panels) made an automobile look menacing and larger than life. Flames became a crutch for mild-mannered rods in the same way that the aggressive designs painted on

World War II fighter planes were used to intimidate the enemy. At the same time, a fiery front end made a car look like it was burning into the atmosphere, like a meteorite—a real plus if you wanted to look fast. (Today, "ghost" flames are all the rage for the understated cruiser.) Still, the burning effect was often nothing more than an illusion, a psychological trick intended to make other customizers and rodders lose faith in their cars.

Not everyone was so insecure when it came to the way their automobiles looked, however. When the cruisin' subculture known as the "lowriders" debuted on the traffic circuits of America, there was no doubting their cars, or their confidence. A product of the *Pachucos*, those flamboyant zoot-suiters of the forties, the first lowriders rolled on the streets of Los Angeles after World War II. As a form of recreation, proud Chicanos dropped the suspensions on their cars, decorated them inside and out, and cruised through the local barrios to display their handiwork. Lowriders added a new book to the American cruisin' bible. Now, the car was more than just an accessory for living, it became synonymous with cultural pride.

By the seventies, this idea of car as symbol of culture took off and suddenly, Latinos across the nation began cutting the coils on favorite cars such

Among cruisers, the fringe group known as "lowriders" finds recreation in cruising their cars extremely close to the ground. By way of chopping tops, cutting springs, and lowering the chassis, vehicles of this genre often possess a defined "rake," the rear of the car being lower than the front. In most cases, the entire car hugs the asphalt to create a low, sinister look. *Mike Witzel*

This 1959 Chevrolet is as low as it can go, creating what some cruisers would call a "weed whacker." In the background sits a classic example of the American filling station, the same sort of outfit that ruled the strip during cruising's golden age. *Kent Bash*

as the 1939 Chevrolet and the 1941 Special Deluxe. Remember the line from War's popular cruisin' ditty: "The lowrider rides a little lower"? Judging the evidence seen on the streets, it was certainly true. The lowrider community took the obsession for appearances down to road level and then beyond.

Everything the custom car had the lowrider had more of. It was lower, slower, and showed a lot more extravagance. Lowriders weren't afraid of using a liberal application of metalflake paint, either. Elaborate murals airbrushed on the trunk lid or body side panels were the rule rather than the exception. On the interior, cars often resembled a bordello on wheels, with fluffy

The showiness extended to the exterior and soon, lowriders became so low that it was difficult for cruisers to navigate the streets properly. About that time, the police started to ticket lowrider owners for illegally lowered suspensions. For many, this looked like the end of lowriding. In fact, it was just the beginning. Cruiser Ron Aguirre got an inspiration: Why not take old aircraft parts and rig up the suspension so that the driver could raise and lower it at will from *inside* the car? The idea sounded crazy, but it worked. After other lowriders saw what the setup could do, the idea of the "lifted" lowrider began to hop—literally! Overnight, lowriders transformed their rides into adjustable street machines! Without worry, they could drive to their favorite cruising venues at the same height as a normal car. When the time came to put on a show, they had the ability to drop it down for maximum effect.

In the final analysis, that's what the art of customizing a car is all about: creativity. Whether an automobile is restyled as wild, mild, low, high, raked, or radical, it's done with the same goal in mind: automotive exhibitionism. With every variation, the activity remains the same. Cruising was and always will be an American folk activity that extracts the very essence of the early coachbuilders, blends it with a need for mobility, folds in a hefty dose of good looks, tosses in a dash of exhibitionism, and shakes the resulting mixture into a delicious treat that many find very palatable.

Who were the kings of custom? You, me, Uncle Joe, your next door neighbor, the tough guy down the street, your school teacher, friends from Europe, Mexican Americans, Australians, African Americans, Asians, that little old lady from Pasadena, Eskimos, anybody qualified. When it came to showing off your personalized car in public, it didn't matter who you were, where you came from, or what color your skin was. The car became a common denominator, the great equalizer. Regardless of social position, everyone was eligible to hold title. All they needed were some wheels and the right attitude to strut their stuff on the streets.

Mouton fur for carpeting and decorative elements that would be at home in a comfortable living room. It wasn't at all unusual for a lowrider to have crushed velvet on the seat covers, pom-pons or tassels decorating the headliner, or a steering wheel made of thick, welded chain. Neon tubes lighting the undercarriage? Only the lowrider could pull it off and get away with it.

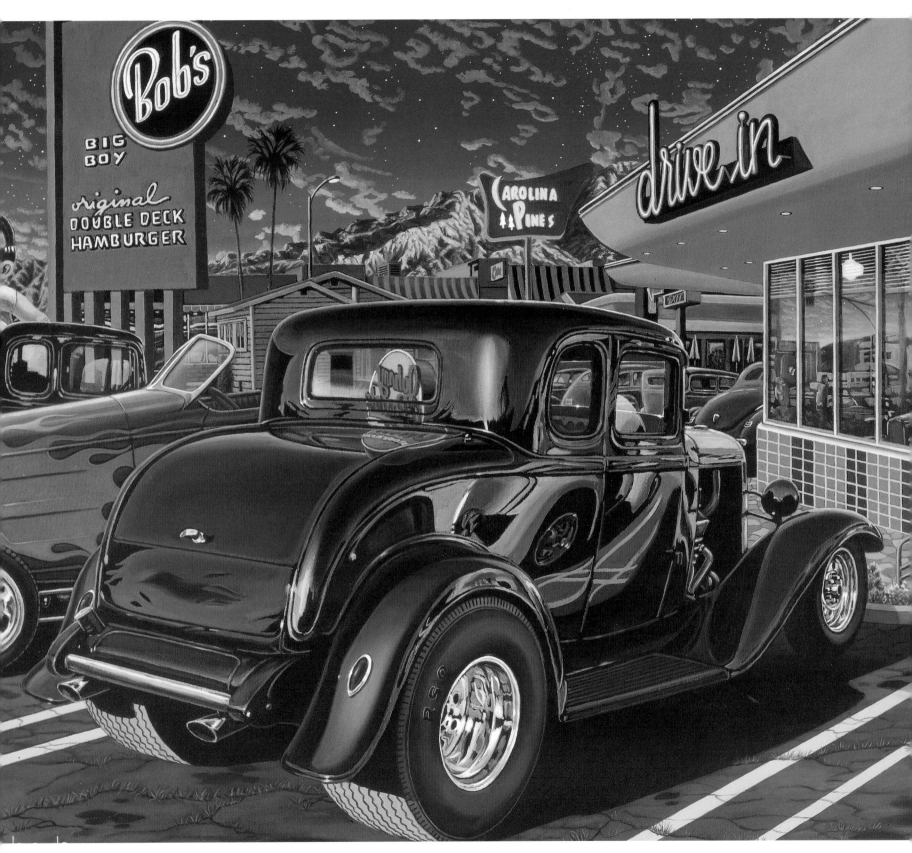

Classic Cruising Strips and Cruise Nights

Taking Back the Streets

"The thing that's attractive about cruise night and something that many people like is that it's spontaneous. Even though there's a date set and there are certain places to go, the thing that's neat about it is that unlike a car show—where people have to sign up, preregister, and pay money—a cruise night is there for you just if you feel like getting out. When the urge to cruise hits, you simply crank up the car and go! The fun of it is that you don't have any idea of who you are going to run into and exactly what's going to happen—other than once everybody's there, you will be hanging around for several hours, visiting, talking, eating, looking around, sharing car stories, and such.

In Southern California, Bob's Big Boy drive-ins were the main destinations for cruisers during the fifties, and with the resurgence of events called "cruise nights," they still are today. Parked and ready for curb service are some of the standards, including a black 1932 five-window coupe, a 1932 roadster with flames, a 1932 coupe, and a 1934 Ford truck. *Kent Bash*

Usually, the parking lot at cruise night is roped off so that only vintage cars, hot rods, muscle cars, customs, or whatever can park in the main area. Once the lot is full, the cars work like a magnet, pulling in people and lookie-lous eager to check out the vehicles and, at the same time, get a quick bite to eat. At Bob's Big Boy in Toluca Lake, comedian Jay Leno shows up every now and then—the place is just a few blocks from the studio where he does the *Tonight Show*. With excitement like this going on, most cruise night restaurants on the West Coast are inundated with customers.

Back in the old days of cruising, during the fifties and the sixties, most drive-in restaurants had car service, so you weren't really able to visit the way you can today. You had to pull your car into a space, order your food, and eat it pretty fast. Only then could you talk to the people in the cars on either side of you, if you knew them. Unlike today, getting out of your car and walking around wasn't cool. Some drive-ins had bouncers or parking people assigned to keep customers in their cars and on the move. Restaurants were in business to make money, and turning over the customers so that new ones could park was all part of it.

Today, a lot of the places that sponsor cruise nights want to give their businesses a shot in the arm. It's easy to do, as organizing a cruise night is not really a big headache unless they plan to spend the extra cash for security or a disc jockey to spin records—which a lot of the better places do. If the place that's sponsoring the event is a good one, there will always be bargains on the food menu and specials for cruisers. At Cruiser's Car Wash in Northridge, California, they have a fifties-style diner inside and serve up both fast food and contemporary dishes. For all the cruisers who don't want to leave their cars and wait inside to get their eats, they set up a barbecue pit in the parking lot and cook tri-tip sandwiches, hot dogs, hot links, and barbecued chicken."
—*Kent Bash*

Chapter Five

IF Woodward Avenue was the Indianapolis of street racing, Van Nuys Boulevard was the melting pot of cruising. It all began in 1912, when horse-drawn carriages still clip-clomped around the village of Van Nuys, California. Every Saturday night, local residents led a parade along Main Street, right through town center. As history tells it, they enjoyed the spectacle so much that they decided to turn the streetfest into a weekly tradition.

After World War II ended, many of the servicemen who shipped into Los Angeles settled down in the valley's residential tracts and continued the ritual. This time, there was a new twist to the cruising: Instead of coaches riding along the dirt, it was motor cars that rumbled down the pavement.

By the end of the fifties, the weekend celebration had grown into an automotive phenomenon. What a radical change had occurred in the San Fernando Valley! From its agricultural past, Van Nuys had grown to see criss-crossing roads replace farms, traffic lights supersede hitching posts, suburban bungalows edge out log cabins, and parking lots replace pastures. The cityscape was now defined by the automobile. The harvest parade enjoyed during olden times was replaced by car-crazed teens in a conspicuous display of personal pride. Carloads of kids converged on Van Nuys Boulevard every Wednesday, Friday, and Saturday night just to cruise up and down the street.

Cruising was such a blast that Van Nuys became the de facto Main Street cruising strip for

The Bob's Big Boy in Canoga Park was once one of the prime cruise night destinations for hot rodders and customizers residing in Los Angeles, California. Now, this former drive-in dining location is just another fond cruising memory. The Bob's Big Boy is gone, and the current owners operate the eatery as just another chain restaurant. Another cruise night bites the dust. *Kent Bash*

most of the surrounding towns. "I first heard my friends talking about the Van Nuys strip in the late fifties and all the action that was going on over there," remembered Cheryl Travers (now a full-time homemaker and mother of three). "I had a nice, white Kaiser-Frazer that my parents helped me purchase when I graduated from high school, and more times than I can recall, me and a few best girlfriends, and sometimes even guy friends, piled into it to cruise up and down the boulevard. Those outings were some of the best times of my entire life!" On Van Nuys, everyone came to see the show and take part in the pageantry, including hot rodders, customizers, mothers in their station wagons, English sports car enthusiasts, families packed in large sedans, lowriders, antique car lovers, limousine drivers, racers in muscle cars, van fans, Volkswagen aficionados, truckers, maniacs on motorcycles, street machine enthusiasts, people in pickup trucks, and many more.

As the fifties sped into the sixties, news of the exuberant street party spread up and down the coast. By the seventies, the strip had gained such notoriety that the phenomenon of cruising overshadowed most street-side business. Not that it was difficult to figure out why: Vehicles crammed with revelers streamed in from cities as far away as San Diego, Santa Barbara, and San Jose. Curiosity seekers streamed in from all over California, boosting the already-swollen crowds to well over 20,000 on the busiest nights! To obtain their vicarious thrills, area residents unfolded lawn chairs on porches and front yards and settled back with a six-pack and popcorn to watch the real-life movie passing by in the street.

Though it was heaven for cruisers, it was hell for merchants. The playful activities enjoyed by the cruisers completely jammed the main business corridor. On the busiest nights when the show was under way, cruisers took over the street and choked the economic life out of it! Crosstown travel or patronage of local businesses was impossible. Regular commuter and shopping traffic couldn't even get into the downtown area much less park anywhere along Van Nuys. To get around the congestion, the traffic department designated alternate access routes just so local residents could get home! "The traffic was pretty slow sometimes," remembered cruiser Cliff Maxwell, a regular denizen of the strip. "Sure, there was a time or two when me and my friends blocked the flow of cars, but it was all just innocent fun. One time,

we staged an elaborate 'turtle race' and lined our cars up with some other ones across one direction of the traffic lanes. Everyone in the bunch drove really slow—about five miles per hour to block traffic behind us. It was a busy night and cars were honking horns and screaming at us to move out of the way. Of course, we didn't clear out until we saw the cherry tops move in. By then, it was too late. Guys that didn't scatter got tickets!"

Out along the miles of boulevard, the huddled masses yearning to cruise free were oblivious to the problems they instigated. On the biggest cruising nights, a spectator could witness plenty of chicanery, including the ubiquitous Chinese Fire Drills (a game where car occupants burst from the doors at a traffic light and run around the vehicle

Cruising down to the local drive-in restaurant was a popular pastime of youth during the fifties and sixties. On almost any night of the week, teenagers (like the now-mature owner of this 1955 Chevrolet) would congregate in great numbers—socializing, eating hamburgers, and tinkering with their cars. It's nice to see that some things never change. *Mike Witzel/cars courtesy Clare Patterson, Jr. and Dan Daniels*

Cleaned up to eliminate all of the hood louvers, rubber on the running boards, and exterior emblems, a 1934 Chevrolet roadster like this example (on its way to a local cruise night event) would be called a "smoothie" by current fans of hot rodding. Adorned with bullet mirrors and digital gauges on the dashboard, these highly refined street rods take the best of the old school and combine it with the best of the new. *Kent Bash*

to change seats, annoying motorists waiting behind), cars bumping other cars, kids popping out of trunks, riders on the outsides of cars, flashing headlamps, musical horns, and lane blocking. "Van Nuys was a crazy scene, man. One time, we were trying to impress some chicks in another car when a friend of mine tossed a beer bottle at their car," explained an avid participant of the time

(who wished to remain anonymous). "It wouldn't have been so bad, but the bottle broke and splattered over the car, making the guy who was driving and his two friends very, very mad. They chased us all over town to beat the tar out of us and finally, we lost 'em. After that, we stored the car in a friend's garage and didn't take it out again for another year. Later, it was sold!" Whether the activities were good, bad, funny, or innocent—if it happened in a car while cruising—it was part of Van Nuys.

Sadly, though perhaps inevitably, all of the endless preening, racing, showing off, and cruising for kicks led to problems. By 1978, serious incidents of crime in Van Nuys proper were up 5 to 10 times on active cruise nights! Two years later, the

Artist Kent Bash created his own form of rolling Volkswagen art during the 1960s, long before the notion of "car art" was an accepted form. To illustrate the theme of "civilization," he finished one side of the vehicle to portray the early stirrings of organized society in the Aztec world. On the flipside, humankind's greatest accomplishments were typified by the yearning for the stars and the conquest of outer space. When it zipped around on the streets, it attracted a lot of interest from the cops and caught the imagination of cruisers up and down the West Coast. © *1997 Steph Butler*

The West Coast Kustoms car club holds cruise night events in the small town of Paso Robles, California, (near the spot where James Dean crashed his car and punched out of this world). The two-day car event has become immensely popular, with Friday night reserved for the obligatory cruise down Main Street over to a parking place at the local A & W drive-in where the parking lot is turned into a car show. *Kent Bash*

Located in Wichita, Kansas, the Kings-X Drive-In holds occasional cruise nights for local enthusiasts. Kings-X got its start in 1938, when the White Castle burger chain decided to close its restaurants west of the Mississippi. Andrew James King was employed by the square burger maker at the time, with 10 years under his belt as head of research and development. As principal "idea-man" for the company, it was his responsibility to develop new products and devise ad promotions. When Billy Ingram announced he was moving Castle's headquarters to Columbus, Ohio, King declined. He bought the three Wichita locations and tried his luck in the burger business. Later, he expanded his holdings, opening Kings-X drive-ins and coffee-shop restaurants in the city. *Mike Witzel*

patience of Van Nuys Boulevard merchants had reached its limit. With an eye toward banning cruising, merchants started bellyaching in earnest about the crowds of juvenile delinquents, the malicious vandalism, and the disgusting incidents of public urination. Ironically, cruisers weren't doing the damage—they remained on the move and inside their cars if at all possible. It was the mob of curious onlookers that was causing most of the mayhem.

Regardless of who was really to blame for all the cruising-related problems, the roadway free-for-all wasn't so amusing anymore. In the eyes of the city leaders, cruising was the root cause of too many transit problems, and with no further debate, it had to go. With that aim in mind, the town organized what it called a police "boulevard detail" in 1983. On the popular cruise nights, the cops cracked down on all drivers who had no destination in mind but were just aimlessly driving up and down the strip. To shunt the free flow of traffic that once electrified the circuit, the patrols erected sawhorse barricades at opposite ends of Van Nuys. Partying crowds who chose to drive across these circuit breakers received citations. Another strategy used warning flares to rip a hole in the night while the boys in blue made mass arrests for public drinking and loitering. Ever so quietly, the department of public works installed signs along the curbside that warned "No Stopping 9 P.M. to 12 Midnight Wednesday–Friday–Saturday." So much for life, liberty, and the pursuit of automotive happiness. . .

The loss of Van Nuys Boulevard as a cruising venue was a tragedy for southern California street enthusiasts, but it was hardly the end of the cruising craze in the United States. Most of America's small-town cruising venues weren't nearly as high-profile as Woodward and Van Nuys, and, as a result, they managed to survive. In spite of the fact that there was an ample number of traffic signs thrown up to ban the activity and plenty of news reports to denounce it, cruisers who maintained low profiles (and remained within the boundaries of the law) could still get in a few good laps on their favorite circuit.

Car enthusiasts believed they had a constitutional right to drive wherever and whenever they wanted, and they weren't going to let a few restrictions stop them. The key was to remain as inconspicuous as possible and never be seen by the black-and-white patrols more than a couple of times per night. And so, clandestine cruising continued into the eighties, and streets that had only recently gotten a reprieve from the dreaded "scourge" actually saw an increase in activity. A law-abiding, low-key, and organized, cruising renaissance had begun.

Cruisin' in the eighties exhibited some distinct differences from the fifties and sixties period—most important, the brash, cavalier attitude of the participants had mellowed. Rather than fall back into the boisterous behavior that had defined cruising during the days of carhops and curb-service, cruisers crossed over into the eighties by adapting to the situation. Automotive hobbyists forgot about fighting the law all the time and

The San Antonio location of the Texas Pig Stands has become a local landmark in the eyes of all those who love the classic steel of the fifties and sixties. With carhops providing service the same way they did 40 years ago (with roller skates), hot rod and muscle car clubs crowd the parking lanes to get a taste of the specialty, barbecued "Pig Sandwiches." ©1997 Louis Persat

decided to work with the police (it got better results when it came to the free expression of their cruising activities and kept their cars from being monitored for illegal equipment). Racing in the streets became a cruising dinosaur. Celebrating wheels for mechanical, aesthetic, and recreational values became the way of the future.

To keep the cruising hobby a vibrant pursuit and to preclude the pointless back and forth runs of yesterday, participants began to hold regularly scheduled get-togethers at nostalgic businesses (cruisers avoided franchised chain outfits). With lit-

Located in Downey, California, Friscos restaurant is one of the hundreds of favorite cruising destinations doing business in the state of California. Wherever you drive in the country, the rules of the cruising game are pretty standard: You park your car, get out, socialize, and chow down on some good old-fashioned American road food. ©1997 Robert Genat

Keller's Drive-In remains as a Dallas, Texas, landmark of car service and cruising. On any night of the week, the serving lanes beneath the canopy are packed with all kinds of customers. Families in station wagons, cowboys in trucks, commuters in sedans, businessmen in Mercedes, and road warriors in hot rods and custom cars—all are welcome at this roadside time machine. Mike Witzel

When vehicles visit a cruise night or other type of automotive show, their drivers often mount car service trays—complete with wax replicas of burger food and milkshakes—to get the feeling back of the way it used to be when cool cars cruised in and out of the many drive-in restaurants. It's a great way to rekindle those fond memories of days gone by and at the same time, a low-fat, low-calorie alternative to real diner fare! *Kent Bash*

tle protest, cruisers agreed that Friday night was to be the prime time for the majority of these roadside rod and custom reunions. On the weekend, surviving restaurants that featured outdoor car service and drive-in theaters that showed movies all night became top destinations to park! Car clubs added their own spin, and each developed its own protocol for taking part in the low-key automotive activities. While the race, creed, and color of the membership varied, one similarity emerged for all: These gas-saving car meets became known as "cruise nights."

The rules and regulations of the typical cruise night are straightforward: First, the members with cars drive to a predetermined spot to hang out for the evening (a place where they have advance approval to park). Often, the destination is a nearby town with businesses that welcome cars and crowds. On the way, the cruisers maintain a respectable decorum and strive to obey the posted speed limit and other related traffic regulations. The members frown upon street racing—as they do reckless driving, practical jokes, and other tomfoolery. Following these guidelines, cruisers have earned a new reputation for themselves, one that's based on public safety and civility. Consider the statement of columnist Tessa DeCarlo in the January 3, 1997, edition of the *Wall Street Journal*: It's her belief that ". . . hot rodding has aged over the last half-century into glossy respectability." With little evidence against them, the majority of modern-day cruisers would agree.

Along old Route 66 in the sleepy town of Seligman, Arizona, Juan Delgadillo and his brother, Angel, have turned their tiny drive-in eatery (and themselves) into a tourist attraction. While Angel runs a small barbershop nearby, Juan feeds the cruisers passing through with the usual roadside fare. For cruisers who make the trek from all parts of the country, stopping in for a quick bite to eat has become a prerequisite. ©1997 Jerry McClanahan

Unlike the adversarial atmosphere of 30 years ago, the modern cruise has grown into a positive win-win situation for all concerned: In exchange for providing automobilists with a gallery to display the mobile manifestations of their imagination, roadside businesses gain an increased visual profile and with it a nice business boost. Proprietors have learned that the cruise night is both an effective way to revitalize a slow operation and supercharge it with new life. Considering the curiosity factor of other car owners, it brings in a lot of extra traffic: "Every time I'm out there cruising, I get mostly positive reactions from those driving regular vehicles. Children wave at me when I pass by, old folks nod their heads at me, and young couples give me the thumbs up," explained Mel Santee, a weekend warrior who likes to check out the local drive-ins in San Francisco, California. "There's just something neat about seeing an old automobile fixed up in a group that brings a twinkle to the eye of commuters. Sometimes, people ask me where I'm going, and then they follow me there!"

And that's precisely what Americans are doing—following the cool cars to nostalgic hot spots! Today, California sets the most visible example: Out on the coast, a mild climate allows residents to enjoy 12 full months of recreational driving. On any given weekend, cruisers may choose from hundreds of venues when the urge comes to park and wolf down a trayful of burgers and fries. Robin Genat listed the most active gathering places in the August 1996 issue of *Westways* magazine. Among her favorite hangouts: Be Bop Burgers in Santa Barbara, EZ Take Out Burger in Acton, Sonic Drive-In at Bakersfield (still using carhop service, Sonic is the only surviving chain of canopy drive-ins in America), the Chicken Pie Diner in Poway, Kooky's Diner and Oscar's over in San Diego, Gigi's Grille in Tustin, Tuxies in Riverside, Hamburger Hank's in Fountain Valley, Heroes Restaurant in Fullerton, Village Grille in Claremont, Bobby's Burgers and Subs in Hemet, Red Robin Burger and Spirits in La Habra, and Frisco's Carhop Drive-In in Downey.

On Tampa Avenue in Northridge, California, Cruiser's Car Wash has become a favorite, providing a squeaky clean backdrop for motorheads eager to park and show off their armor. Washing work is done on the premises, but no respectable cruiser allows another to clean his or her hot rod or custom. The Toluca Lake Bob's Big Boy is a favorite destination. (In the old days the Glendale Bob's on Colorado Boulevard and the Van Nuy's location were infamous hangouts.) During the early nineties, the Toluca Lake location survived demolition by way of cruiser outrage.

In St. John, Missouri, the Chuck-A-Burger has been hosting cruisers since 1957. The restaurant still provides curb service, as well as a dining room and carry-out service. A future cruiser takes heed of the bold Chuck-A-Burger drive-in sign. ©1997 Shellee Graham

The Road Kings club was instrumental in saving the 43-year-old building. Later, the city designated the landmark as an official California Point of Historical Interest. Today, it's a strong pull for customs and retro fifties characters who want to relive a slice of time they were never really a part of. Management is happy for the extra business and the notoriety.

Recently, some of the small towns in the Golden State have begun to organize street fairs combined with automobile shows on the weekends. Rod and custom shows (with every other kind of car mixed in between) have popped up in locales like San Bernardino, Pismo Beach, Temecula, and Long Beach. Now, instead of banning cruising and the large gathering of cars that go with it, cities have discovered it's a good way to step up tourism and give commerce a shot in the arm. Some cities allow visitors to cruise down Main on a special night with uncorked headers (the cops turn their heads the other way)! In Paso Robles, near the site of the James Dean accident, the West Coast Kustoms hold a custom car show during Labor Day weekend every year. The town closes down regular traffic on Friday night and cruisers take over the street. Afterwards, the local A & W drive-in caters to all participants with fried foods and car service. It's literally a blast from the past.

All over America, there's a similar flurry of activity: A weekly meeting of classic cars in St. Paul, Minnesota, transforms the University Avenue strip into a jam-packed parking lot. Into the wee hours of the morning, hot rods and custom cars flash their toothy, chrome grins beneath the glowing neon of Porky's Drive-In.

While this 1940 Ford Sedan could be classified as a fifties-style rod, the tuck-and-roll upholstery inside definitely marks it as a custom job. Out-of-the-way roadside joints like Oink's are where many of today's car guys hang out—if they can find them. Fast food operations have forever changed the way mobile America eats. Many of the quaint spots of the fifties are now extinct. *Kent Bash*

Deep down in Texas, a club that calls itself the Cruzin' Cruisers reserves every third weekend in September for an automobile show and drive-in theater pilgrimage. Similarly, the Texas Pig Stand drive-in in Beaumont (the oldest remaining round drive-in diner in the United States) regularly sees its share of cruising activity—as does its sister outlet in San Antonio. Nearby in Waco, the Heart of Texas Street Machines (a mix of rods, customs, muscle cars, and other classics) makes the Healthcamp drive-in the fifties flashback of choice every third Tuesday of the month.

At the same time, the "Old Town" area of Kissimmee, Florida, erupts into what some locals describe as cruising mania: Every Saturday night,

hoards of vintage vehicles converge on the tiny hamlet to vie for street space. Up and down the East Coast, it's the same story, only the names of the eateries have changed. In Churchville, Maryland, the Big M Drive-In Restaurant beckons the tuck-and-roll crowd to stoke up on fun food and films. Distilfink, one of Pennsylvania's favorite drive-ins, tempts the customers cruising in convertibles and Cadillacs to grab a bit of grub in the town of Gettysburg. Out on Long Island, muscle car maniacs (who once raced their street machines up and down Deer Park Avenue) jockey for a good space at Carmichael's. Up north in Connecticut, Mickey's provides East Hartford cruisers a visible place to park and chow down an oversized slice of cruising pie. Regardless of locality—be it a small town or large, a region in the North, East, South, or West—cruise night is a duplicated franchise.

Nationwide, cruise night participants enjoy similar activities. One of the most common rituals is to check out the automobiles in attendance for their strengths and weaknesses. To facilitate this once-

Wednesday and Saturday night have become the accepted times for the cruisers to huddle together at the drive-in restaurants of America. ©1997 Robert Genat

The Paso Robles Custom Car Show, organized by the West Coast Customs, exists as a great excuse to take out the custom beauty and cruise it on over to the local A & W drive-in. *Kent Bash*

over, it's best for cruisers to park with nose facing out, in the direction of the audience (it's a must to raise the hood and display the engine). Then, participants are free to leave their automobile and break out the California duster, a cleaning tool used to remove dust particles. Afterwards, they might mingle or strike up conversation with old friends or new. As expected, the car becomes the main point of conversation and mechanical stories the topic. There's a lot of "bench racing" too, a pastime where

racing exploits are retold for those unlucky enough not to be in attendance when they happened. Like the fishing stories about the "whopper that got away," cruisers like to stretch the truth.

But even though no one is really racing with cars these days, the aspect of competition isn't totally extinct at cruise nights. Static events are the new kick and, sometimes, loosely organized contests determine the best-looking street machine or the most radically altered custom. On some occasions,

when the organizers and venues allow it, burnout contests celebrate the cruiser who can generate the most tire smoke! Other times, cruise nights are an interesting mix of subdued sideshow events like dance contests, fifties fashion shows, and food-making festivals. (At one recent gathering, organizers tempted cruisers to enter the biggest beehive hairdo contest.) Although taking part in the fun is the primary impetus, winners usually come away with a prize.

With prizes in mind, a standby that attracts a big cruise night crowd is the raffle. Upon arrival, the ringleaders ask the cruisers (and visitors who come to drool over the vintage tin) to toss a buck into a pot and, in exchange, they hand out tickets. As the cruise night activities unfold, the crowd is free to check out the array of prizes displayed on tables for all to see. At the end of the evening's festivities, a series of drawings determines the lucky winners who will cruise home with stuff like automotive

The raised hood is perhaps the most common sight at the modern-day cruise night. With that in mind, one of the most common pastimes is talking about one's car. After that, bench racing and talking about past street (or drag) racing competitions comes in a close second. ©1997 Robert Genat

cleaning supplies, speed parts, and other cool accessories. When it's not an actual prize that's put up for grabs, the motor club donates the collected money to a good cause or local charity.

To the credit of the rod and custom crowd, a lot of car clubs hold cruise events for the sole purposes of raising cash, gathering canned goods, collecting Christmas gifts, and increasing public awareness.

And—as much as today's calorie-counting cruisers hate to admit it—another important element of cruise night that attracts interest is food. Is it merely a coincidence that cruisers hold car events at restaurants that specialize in junk food served up fast? It's probably by design, as the weekly reprieve

At the 1995 Route 66 Rendezvous in the city of San Bernardino, California, a total of 190,000 visitors took the "highway that's the best" and followed in the tracks of Buz and Tod. There, a 15-block stretch of the "Mother Road" became a playground for rods, customs, and other street machines. ©1997 Robert Genat

Cruising the Main Street strip is alive and well in the California town of Paso Robles. The West Coast Kustoms car club regularly takes over the central traffic corridor of town. It's all perfectly legal—the boys in blue are held in check during the event. Only normal traffic violations are prohibited. *Kent Bash*

There's nothing that's more appealing than getting together a bunch of friends and cruising the local strip in a convertible. The wind in your hair, the sounds on the radio, and the happy reactions of onlookers are just a few of the things that make it a worthwhile outing. ©1997 Robert Genat

Caught in mid-cruise at a busy intersection, this bold, hot yellow Chevrolet was just one of the many colorful sights and sounds seen at the Route 66 Rendezvous held in San Bernardino, California. ©1997 Robert Genat

from the suburban dinner table provides cholesterol watchers an excuse to skip the tofu-and-sprouts routine. With racing activities banned and roadway antics barred, there must be a few indulgences left that car fans may enjoy guilt-free, even if artery-glue is part of the package! Yes, the double-deck cheeseburger, the greasy french fries, the onion rings, the milkshakes mixed up with real milk, the banana splits, old-fashioned tubesteaks (slathered with chili and onions), and mugs of sweet root beer (consuming alcohol while cruising is frowned upon) are now staple cruising foods.

With the appetite satisfied, cruise nighters invariably turn their ears toward music and entertainment. In that department, a sound system or portable disc jockey arrangement become the focal point. At the best events, it's just like American Bandstand. The only differences are that 45-rpm

A parking lot full of cars would normally be a pretty mundane sight, except for when its cruise night in Tacoma, Washington. Then, the usual, mundane, everyday commuter cars are replaced with cool hot rods, muscle cars, customs, lowriders, and much more. ©1997 Robert Genat

Frank Redford's classic Wigwam motels have worked their way into the roadside culture of America and are favorite destinations for cruisers traveling Route 66, the old Mother Road. Every now and then, these motels from the past can be seen hosting visitors who arrive in cars like this 1937 Chevrolet and 1954 Buick Skylark convertible (it was Buick's 50th anniversary car). The Buick is a fine example of a car no customizer would dare change. It was perfect right off the showroom floor. *Kent Bash*

records are no longer used (it's mostly compact discs these days), and a weekend disc-jockey or local radio personality plays the part of Dick Clark. The hit parade of the good old days again holds sway, and the favorite tunes of the forties, fifties, and sixties are cruise night standards. It's appropriate that many of the radio stations that follow this same sort of nostalgia play list are also part of the cruise night concert. With little exception, they engage in cross-promotion with cruise night organizers and the venues hosting the event.

Yet, despite all of the media attention and air play, national gatherings still manage to overshadow local and regional cruises. Using the small-town cruise night as the model, major car events allow the avid cruiser an opportunity to see a lot more than the local Tastee Freeze parking lot can offer. Drawing crowds of up to 10,000, the annual Hot August Nights in Reno, Nevada, is the typical meet. Similarly, the highly publicized Americruise convenes every year, allowing cruisers to select from eight tours and to begin each one of them from starting points in various states. Highway nostalgia is now a major draw, too. At the 1995 Route 66 Rendezvous in the city of San Bernardino, California, a total of 190,000 visitors took the

The car grille: ever since the first American motor carriage rolled off the assembly line, it's exhibited some sort of human-like quality and personality. It's the metallic faces of the forties and fifties cars (like this Buick Eight), however, that are imbued with the most outrageous personalities. Perhaps that's why the modern cruise night is such a friendly, fun activity. *Mike Witzel*

Although many drive-ins welcome cruisers on planned cruise nights, there are times when idle driving is frowned upon. This Steak n Shake on Route 66 in Springfield, Missouri, welcomes nostalgia seekers, but discourages loitering in the parking lot. ©*1997 Shellee Graham*

"highway that's the best" and followed in the tracks of Buz and Tod. There, a 15-block stretch of the "Mother Road" through San Bernardino became a playground for rods, customs, and other street machines. Some 1,200 vehicles joined vintage Corvettes, just like the one seen in the classic television program *Route 66*, to cruise Main.

Recently, muscle car fans enjoyed their own special cruising event: In August 1995, local cities, businesses, and car clubs in Detroit, Michigan, started up the first Woodward Avenue Dream Cruise. Three days before the event, motor homes, travel trailers, and car-haulers from all over

The "blessing of the cars" has become a tradition at many automobile shows and cruise events in southern California. This priest arrived on a skateboard then donned a flamed robe. Men of the cloth are frequently on hand to praise God and pray for the safety and good fortune of the cruisers and for good clear weather. Ironically, it's the car that has become the new religion for many Americans. The real question for theologians to ponder is this: If Jesus came back tomorrow, would he be a hot rodder, customizer, lowrider, muscle car driver—or all four? *Courtesy Fred DuPuis*

While cruising where one can be seen is the status quo, the long-distance jaunt into the country is a favorite activity among many automobile clubs and cruising fans. The call of the open highway, the lure of the unknown destination, and the journey itself are all part of the experience. A blue 1940 Chevy and a flamed 1940 Plymouth are shown here, parked but ready to roll. *Kent Bash*

America descended on the four-lane strip. Local restaurants got into the spirit and charged the same prices they had in 1966. Believe it or not, an estimated 250,000 people showed up and 10,000 to 15,000 cars turned the former muscle car strip into a parking lot. One lap around the Woodward circuit took two hours! Sock hops, car shows, movies, burnout contests, and the lure of cruising back in time packed the traffic lanes with memories. Attendees who took part in the main run got

to take a bit of memorabilia home with them: Each of the six host cities gave out a dash plaque shaped like a puzzle piece. Cruisers who made the complete run collected all of the pieces and assembled them to make one big commemorative plaque.

Along with muscle cars, every conceivable type of car slipped along Motor City's most prominent street, including funky lowriders, way-out hot rods, speedy dragsters, and customized lead sleds. But it was more than just a blast from the past: The presence

In Buellton, California, remnants of yesterday's roadside eateries provide the perfect, real-life backdrop for artist Kent Bash's T-bucket roadster. On long-distance cruise events, nostalgic scenes like this one are a resounding favorite with participants. This 1925 Ford is packed with a Buick nailhead engine (big-block 401) and features American mag wheels on a shortened and narrowed 1932 Ford frame. The beer keg gas tank is a popular fuel format for the hot rodder and used most often with the open-bodied T configuration. *Kent Bash*

Without argument, the philosophy of what a car should look like has come a long way from the day when it took four weeks to paint a Ford. With the Model T, body parts were sanded and painted five times with days of drying left between each coat. Because black pigment dried quickest, it became *the* default assembly line color. Fortunately, the drab standard was dropped—and future rod and custom builders liberated—when chemists at Dupont developed an improved lacquer that dried in two hours! General Motors was the first to use the formula on the "True Blue" Oakland Six in 1924. As the nation entered the Great Depression, cars mirrored the somber situation of the times and stylists used reserved shades of brown, blue, green, and maroon. It wasn't until after World War II that the depressing hues were lightened. Today, hot rod colors are loud, bold, and vibrant! ©1997 *Robert Genat*

In California, Johnny Carson Park (within walking distance of NBC studios) is a favorite place for the car club known as the Road Kings to hold some of their major car events. Started during the late forties, the Road Kings hosts a diverse membership of rod and custom fans, and today the club continues to sponsor a number of worthwhile automotive events in the region. *Kent Bash*

of brand new motoring forms (and diverse participants) signaled that the cruising phenomenon in this country is alive and well. In fact, it's spinning off entirely new breeds. From the sort of vehicles spied in the street, it became painfully obvious that buying a replica body of formed fiberglass is

now acceptable hot rod behavior. At the same time, present-day hot rodders and customizers have the choice of fashioning their ride the way they did during the fifties, or they may return to the standards of the thirties and forties. Even lowriders looked different; suddenly, the act of lifting a chassis appeared passé. Case in point: those mini-trucks with elaborate hydraulics. Instead of controlling the suspension, the truck bed is now the object of all gyration.

Whether the hot rod and custom purists like it or not, the types of cars the next generation is choosing for cruising coaches are changing. For today's neophyte unfamiliar with the automotive arts of the golden age, it's perfectly acceptable to take a car like an Acura Integra (or other import) and transform it into a cruiser. In a trend that's alarming traditionalists, tried-and-true marques like Chevy, Ford, and Mercury are being "dissed" in favor of smaller, less imposing types of compacts including Honda Civics and CRXs, Nissan Sentras, Mitsubishi 3000 GTs, and others. The kids who don baggy shorts, backward baseball caps, and stubby goatees spend piles of cash on the sorts of automobiles that the cruising enthusiasts of old wouldn't give a second glance. Now, in addition to engine and body modifications, it's those booming, high-power audio systems that get all the attention! Overpowered stereo amplifiers and trunk-mounted subwoofers have replaced the hand-tuned flathead as the symbol of male bravado. Supposedly, the more power and higher the volume level the mobile generation X'er can sustain, the more respect he gains.

To be fair, the old-timers of cruising's golden age shouldn't be so hard on the upstarts fighting for a parking place along the mean streets of America. After all, even today's average motorist has little in common with the car owner of the early 20th century: Locked within a soundproof cocoon of lightweight sheet metal and composites, one may recline in the comfort of four-way adjustable seats, glide down the interstate with cruise-control, monitor traffic conditions with a heads-up display, enjoy speed-sensitive steering, engage anticollision radar, groove to the sounds of compact disc music, verify

directions with a global positioning satellite and computer display, conduct conversations by cellular telephone, and even send (or receive) fax transmissions en route.

Further advancements promise to widen the technology gap even more. Aided by a digital computer and external sensors, the next generation of advanced motor vehicles will possess the ability to regulate their own speed of travel and safely guide themselves along controlled paths (engineers played with "automatic highways" as early as the fifties). Efficient motors powered by innovative energy sources will render the gasoline engine and its peripheral equipment obsolete. Compact powerplants fueled by new sources of energy are leaving the realm of science-fiction and entering the arena of practicality. With each passing decade, the gas-guzzling carriages of antiquity roll toward a future devoid of petroleum.

So, is cruising on the way out? Probably not. Even if radical environmentalists confiscate all of the automobiles and government bureaucrats outlaw all fossil fuel engines, car lovers will find entirely new ways to take a ride down the Main Street strip and show off their personalities. It doesn't matter if that new source of energy is hydrogen, solar panels, rechargeable batteries, cold fusion, nuclear fission, dilithium crystal, or flux capacitor. As long as this nation remains free, motorists will never give up their cars and the recreational outlet they provide without a fight. While walking may be good for health and flying in an airplane a safer way to travel, there's nothing quite so satisfying as strapping yourself into the bucket seat of a gorgeous convertible, cranking the ignition switch, throwing the four-on-the-floor shifter into gear, popping the clutch, pressing your foot against the accelerator pedal, slipping your arm around your date, grooving to the tunes on the radio, checking out the scene, and indulging yourself in the passion called Cruisin'.

Recommended Back-Seat Reading

Barris, George, and David Fetherston. *Barris Kustoms of the 1950s*. Osceola, Wisconsin: Motorbooks International, 1994.

Batchelor, Dean. *The American Hot Rod*. Osceola, Wisconsin: Motorbooks International, 1995.

Benjaminson, James A. *Plymouth 1946–1959*. Osceola, Wisconsin: Motorbooks International, 1994.

Boyer, William P. *Thunderbird: An Odyssey in Automotive Design*. Dallas, Texas: Taylor Publishing Company, 1986.

Boyne, Walter J. *Power Behind the Wheel: Creativity and Evolution of the Automobile*. New York: Stewart, Tabori and Chang, 1988.

Brown, Lester R., Christopher Flavin, and Colin Norman. *Running on Empty: the Future of the Automobile in an Oil Short World*. New York: W. W. Norton and Company, 1979.

Campisano, Jim. *American Muscle Cars*. New York: Metro Books, 1995.

Dauphinais, Dean, and Peter M. Gareffa. *Car Crazy: The Official Motor City High-Octane, Turbocharged, Chrome-Plated, Back Road Book of Car Culture*. Detroit, Michigan: Visible Ink Press, 1996.

Drake, Albert. *Beyond the Pavement*. Adelphi, Maryland: The White Ewe Press, 1981.

Drake, Albert. *Street Was Fun in '51*. Okemos, Michigan: Flat Out Press, 1982.

Egan, Philip S. *Design and Destiny: the Making of the Tucker Automobile*. Orange, California: On the Mark Publications, 1989.

Fetherston, David. *Heroes of Hot Rodding*. Osceola, Wisconsin: Motorbooks International, 1992.

Fetherston, David. *Hot Rod Memorabilia and Collectibles*. Osceola, Wisconsin: Motorbooks International, 1996.

Finch, Christopher. *Highways to Heaven: The Auto Biography of America*. New York: HarperCollins Publishers Inc., 1992.

Flink, James J. *The Automobile Age*. Cambridge, Massachusetts: The MIT Press, 1988.

Flink, James J. *The Car Culture*. Cambridge, Massachusetts: The MIT Press, 1975.

Ganahl, Pat. *Hot Rods and Cool Customs*. New York: Abbeville Press, 1993.

Gelderman, Carol. *Henry Ford: The Wayward Capitalist*. New York: St. Martin's Press, 1981.

Gunnel, John A., and Mary L. Sieber. *The Fabulous Fifties: The Cars, The Culture*. Iola, Wisconsin: Krause Publications, 1992.

Heat Moon, William Least. *Blue Highways: A Journey Into America*. Boston: Atlantic Monthly Press, 1982.

Hirsch, Jay. *Great American Dream Machines: Classic Cars of the 50s and 60s*. New York: Macmillan Publishing Company, 1985.

Hoffman, Robert N. *Murder on the Highway*. New York: A. S. Barnes and Company Inc., 1966.

Horsley, Fred. *Hot Rod It—and Run for Fun! How to Build and Operate a Hot Rod Safely*. Englewood Cliffs, New Jersey: Prentice-Hall Inc., 1957.

Ikuta, Yasutoshi. *Cruise O Matic: Automobile Advertising of the 1950s*. San Francisco, California: Chronicle Books, 1988.

Jewell, Derek. *Man & Motor: The 20th Century Love Affair*. New York: Walker and Company, 1966.

Keller, Ulrich. *The Highway as Habitat: A Roy Stryker Documentation, 1943–1955*. Santa Barbara, California: University Art Museum, 1986.

Kerouac, Jack. *On the Road*. New York: Viking Penguin, 1955.

Kitahara, Teruhisa. *Cars: Tin Toy Dreams*. San Francisco: Chronicle Books, 1985.

Lawlor, John. *How to Talk Car*. Chicago, Illinois: Topaz Felson Books, 1965.

Leffingwell, Randy. *American Muscle: Muscle Cars from the Otis Chandler Collection*. Osceola, Wisconsin: Motorbooks International, 1990.

Lent, Henry B. *The Automobile–U.S.A.: Its Impact on People's Lives and the National Economy*. New York: E. P. Dutton and Company Inc., 1968.

Lewis, David L., and Lawrence Goldstein. *The Automobile and American Culture*. Ann Arbor: The University of Michigan Press, 1980.

Matteson, Donald W. *The Auto Radio, A Romantic Genealogy*. Jackson, Michigan: Thornridge Publishing, 1987.

Montgomery, Don. *Hot Rods in the Forties: A Blast from the Past*. Fallbrook, California: Don Montgomery, 1987.

Don Montgomery. *Supercharged Gas Coupes*. Fallbrook, California: Don Montgomery, 1993.

Mueller, Mike. *Chevy Muscle Cars*. Osceola, Wisconsin: Motorbooks International, 1994.

Mike Mueller. *Fifties American Cars*. Osceola, Wisconsin: Motorbooks International, 1994.

Nader, Ralph. *Unsafe at Any Speed*. New York: Grossman Publishers, 1972.

Newton, Kenneth, W. Steeds, and T. K. Garrett. *The Motor Vehicle*. London, England: Butterworth-Heinemann Ltd., 1991.

O'Brien, Richard. *The Story of American Toys*. New York: Abbeville Press, 1990.

Oppel, Frank. *Motoring in America: The Early Years*. Secaucus, New Jersey: Castle Books, 1989.

Oyslager Organisation. *American Cars of the 1960s*. London, England: Frederick Warne Ltd., 1977.

Packard, Chris. *Safe Driving*. New York: J. B. Lippincott Company, 1974.

Pearce, Christopher. *Fifties Sourcebook: A Visual Guide to the Style of a Decade*. Secaucus, New Jersey: Chartwell Books, 1990.

Petersen Publishing Company. *The Best of Hot Rod*. Los Angeles, California: Petersen Publishing Company, 1986.

Post, Robert C. *High Performance: The Culture and Technology of Drag Racing 1950–1990*. Baltimore, Maryland: The John Hopkins University Press, 1994.

Roth, Ed "Big Daddy," and Tony Thacker. *Hot Rods by Ed "Big Daddy" Roth*. Osceola, Wisconsin: Motorbooks International, 1995.

Segrave, Kerry. *Drive-in Theaters, A History from Their Inception in 1933*. Jefferson, North Carolina: McFarland and Company Inc., 1992.

Seiffert, Ulrich, and Peter Walzer. *Automobile Technology of the Future*. Warrendale, Pennsylvania: The Society of Automotive Engineers, 1989.

Silk, Gerald, Angelo Anselmi, Henry Robert Jr., and Strother MacMinn. *Automobile and Culture*. New York: Harry N. Abrams Inc., 1984.

Smith, Dan. *Accessory Mascots: The Automotive Accents of Yesteryear, 1910–1940*. San Diego, California: Dan Smith Publishing, 1989.

Smith, Mark, and Naomi Black. *America on Wheels: Tales and Trivia of the Automobile*. New York: William Morrow and Company Inc., 1986

Society for Commercial Archeology. *The Automobile in Design and Culture*. Edited by Jan Jennings. Ames: Iowa State University Press, 1990.

Southard, Andy. *Custom Cars of the 1950s*. Osceola, Wisconsin: Motorbooks International, 1993.

Stambler, Irwin. *The Supercars and the Men Who Race Them*. New York: G. P. Putnam's Sons, 1975.

Steinbeck, John. *The Grapes of Wrath*. New York: The Viking Press, 1939.

Steinbeck, John. *Travels with Charley*. New York: The Viking Press, 1962.

Time-Life Books. *This Fabulous Century, 1920–1930*. New York: Time-Life Books, 1969.

Williams, William C. *Motoring Mascots of the World*. Portland, Oregon: Graphic Arts Center Publishing, 1990.

Wilson, Paul. *Chrome Dreams: Automobile Styling Since 1893*. Radnor, Pennsylvania: Chilton Book Company, 1976.

Wilson, Richard Guy, Dianne H. Pilgrim, and Dickran Tashjian. *The Machine Age in America 1918–1941*. New York: Harry N. Abrams Inc., 1986.

Witzel, Michael Karl. *The American Drive-In: History and Folklore of the Drive-In Restaurant in American Car Culture*. Osceola, Wisconsin: Motorbooks International, 1994.

Witzel, Michael Karl. *The American Gas Station: History and Folklore of the Gas Station in American Car Culture*. Osceola, Wisconsin: Motorbooks International, 1992.

Witzel, Michael Karl. *Drive-In Deluxe*. Osceola, Wisconsin: Motorbooks International, 1997.

Witzel, Michael Karl. *Gas Station Memories*. Osceola, Wisconsin: Motorbooks International, 1994.

Witzel, Michael Karl. *Route 66 Remembered*. Osceola, Wisconsin: Motorbooks International, 1996.

Young, Anthony, and Mike Mueller. *Chevrolet's Hot Ones*. Osceola, Wisconsin: Motorbooks International, 1995.

Index